vital vegetables

vital
vegetables

Edited by Orlando Murrin

SOMA

Text © The contributors 1999
Photography © The photographers 1999
(For a full list of contributors and
photographers see page 156)
Design & Layout © 1999 Quadrille
Publishing Limited

First published 1999 in Great Britain by
BBC Worldwide Ltd. Designed and produced
by Quadrille Publishing Ltd. North American
edition published 1999 by Soma Books,
by arrangement with Quadrille

Soma Books is an imprint of Bay Books &
Tapes, 555 De Haro St., No. 220,
San Francisco, CA 94107

For the Quadrille edition:
Editor & Project Manager: Lewis Esson
Editorial Director: Jane O'Shea
Art Director: Mary Evans
Design: Paul Welti & Coralie Bickford-Smith
North American Editor:
Editorial Assistant: Caroline Perkins
Project Editor for the BBC: Vicki Vrint
Production: Julie Hadingham

For the Soma edition:
North American Editors: Beverly Le Blanc
and Andrea Chesman

Library of Congress Cataloging-in-Publication
Data on file with the Publisher

ISBN 1-57959-059-4

Printed and bound in Singapore
by KHI Printing Co Pte Ltd
Color separations by Colourscan, Singapore
Distributed by Publishers Group West

Throughout the book, recipes serve four
unless otherwise indicated

contents

6 INTRODUCTION

8 TAKING STOCK
Soups, Stocks, and Sauces

24 MAKING OVERTURES
Appetizers, Snacks, and Light
Meals

64 PUTTING ON THE HEAT
Bakes, Gratins, Pies, and Tarts

90 MAKE IT MEDITERRANEAN
Pasta, Pizza, Risotto, etc.

114 STAPLE DIET
Ways with Potatoes

134 STIRRING IT UP
Asian Ways with Vegetables

146 FESTIVE BITES
Party Food

156 ACKNOWLEDGMENTS

158 INDEX

introduction

Vegetables have undergone a radical repositioning in our cooking over the last decade—from being the stalwart reliable background fillers in our meals to all-singing, all-dancing leading roles in all courses.

Of course, vegetarians have been giving them star billing for some time now, and their influence—combined with the influence of Mediterranean, especially Italian, cuisine on our culture—has spread so widely that there is now an almost universal acceptance that meals no longer need to consist of "meat and two vegetables." Exciting and tasty vegetable dishes are enjoyed these days by everyone, even nonvegetarians who never expected to relish meals that are meat-free.

In this lavish new cookbook, you will find over 200 original recipes and ideas for a vast range of mouthwatering ways with vegetables—some so simple they can be made in a matter of minutes for a quick snack, appetizer, or appealing side dish; others so spectacular or inspired they are guaranteed to have friends or family sitting up and taking notice. There are dishes for all occasions, budget levels, and all seasons—including many that can be made entirely, or in part, ahead of time.

The recipes have been devised by a constellation of masterful chefs and food writers from across Europe and are presented here by noted food writer Orlando Murrin. Every recipe is fully tested, and a wealth of splendid photographs shows just how good vegetable dishes can look. Most chapters include at least one feature on a particular vegetable–either an old favorite, such as the potato, or a relative unknown like the Jerusalem artichoke—crammed with information on how to choose, store, and prepare the vegetables so that you can buy and cook them with more confidence.

Because everything is explained with such care and expertise, in a clear and user-friendly way, it makes no difference whether you are a beginner or an experienced cook; this book has a place on every kitchen shelf.

Among the most comforting of dishes are soups made from masses of tasty vegetables, be they nourishing clear broths or thick, hearty purees. At their heart usually lies a flavor-packed vegetable stock, which can also form the basis for many classic sauces. Soups also provide an opportunity to experiment with new combinations of vegetables, flavorings, and spices.

Taking Stock

Soups, Stocks, and Sauces

Spicy Gazpacho with Basil

This simple chilled Spanish soup cropped up on many menus in the '60s and '70s.

PREPARATION: 15 MINUTES,
PLUS 2 HOURS CHILLING
SERVES 6 TO 8

Generous 1 cup extra-virgin olive oil

1 red onion, chopped

2 garlic cloves, minced

1 red bell pepper, seeded and chopped

4 ripe tomatoes, chopped

2 slices white bread, roughly torn

1 (14 ounce) can tomatoes pureed with
   their juices

4 tablespoons white wine vinegar

1 teaspoon hot pepper sauce

1¼ cups vegetable stock

1 teaspoon sugar

Salt and pepper

Handful basil leaves, to garnish

1 Pour ⅔ cup extra-virgin olive oil into an ice-cube tray and freeze.

2 Put the onion, garlic, bell pepper, ripe tomatoes, and bread into a food processor and blend until finely chopped but not too smooth—you need to keep some of the crunchy texture.

3 Transfer to a large bowl with the pureed tomatoes. Add 5 tablespoons of the remaining oil, the vinegar, hot pepper sauce, stock, sugar, and salt and pepper to taste; remember, food to be served chilled needs to be strongly seasoned. Mix thoroughly, cover the bowl with plastic wrap, and chill for at least 2 hours or overnight. You can prepare ahead up to this point.

4 Just before serving, pour the soup into serving bowls. Drop a couple of frozen olive-oil cubes into each, and drizzle with a little more oil. Tear some basil leaves over each bowl and serve.

Caldo Verde

This traditional Portuguese soup is a great way of using up leftover vegetables.

PREPARATION: 10 MINUTES,
PLUS OVERNIGHT SOAKING
COOKING: 1¼ HOURS
SERVES 4

½ cup dried cannellini beans

1 tablespoon olive oil

1 onion, chopped

2 garlic cloves, crushed

1 large potato, diced

2 large fresh sage leaves, shredded

About 2½ cups shredded Savoy cabbage

2 cups vegetable stock

Salt and pepper

1 Soak the beans overnight in cold water.

2 Drain the beans and then put in a large pan with 5 cups cold water. Bring to a boil and boil rapidly for 10 minutes. Remove any foam with a slotted spoon. Reduce the heat and simmer for 40 minutes, or until the beans are tender.

3 Meanwhile, heat the oil in a pan. Add the onion and garlic, and sauté for 5 minutes until soft. Stir in the potato and sage, and sauté for 5 minutes longer, stirring occasionally.

4 Stir the onion mixture into the beans, together with the cabbage and stock. Bring to a boil. Lower the heat and simmer for 15 minutes, stirring occasionally. Season to taste. Serve with crusty bread.

Chinese Broth with Curly Kale Seaweed

PREPARATION: 15 MINUTES

COOKING: 40 MINUTES

SERVES 4

2 garlic cloves, chopped

2 lemongrass stalks, chopped

1-inch piece fresh ginger root, chopped

5 scallions, sliced

1 red chile, seeded and chopped

$6^{1}/_{4}$ cups vegetable stock

1 tablespoon chile or olive oil

$^{1}/_{2}$ cup baby corn, halved lengthwise

2 small carrots, cut into matchsticks

$1^{1}/_{2}$ cups shredded kale

$1^{1}/_{2}$ cups quartered button mushrooms

8 ounces fresh Chinese noodles, or 4 ounces dried

1 tablespoon dry sherry

2 tablespoons soy sauce

2 tablespoons lime juice

Vegetable oil for frying

Salt and pepper

1 Place the garlic, lemongrass, ginger, scallions, and chile in a food processor and blend to a coarse paste. Heat the stock in a pan with the paste until boiling. Lower the heat, cover, and simmer for 30 minutes.

2 Meanwhile, heat the chile or olive oil in a wok or large skillet. Add the corn, carrots, $1^{1}/_{4}$ cups of the kale and cook for 5 minutes until soft. Add the mushrooms and stock mixture, and cook for 3 minutes longer. Add the noodles and cook for 2 minutes (4 if using dried noodles). Stir in the sherry, soy sauce, and lime juice, and simmer for 1 minute longer. Season to taste.

3 Heat about $^{3}/_{4}$ inch vegetable oil in a skillet. Add a little of the remaining kale to the pan. If it sizzles, the oil is hot enough. Add the rest of the remaining kale and fry for a few seconds. Remove with a slotted spoon and drain on paper towels; it should become crisp.

4 Serve broth and noodles in bowls, topped with crisp kale.

Spiced Lentil Soup with Lemon Yogurt

PREPARATION: 15 MINUTES

COOKING: 50 MINUTES

SERVES 4

Sprig each of fresh parsley, cilantro, and thyme

1 celery stalk

3 tablespoons olive oil

2 onions, chopped

2 carrots, chopped

5 garlic cloves, roughly chopped

1 tablespoon ground cumin

1 tablespoon paprika

2 teaspoons ground turmeric

$2^1/_2$ cups French lentils

$2^1/_2$ quarts vegetable stock

Juice of $^1/_2$ lemon

$^2/_3$ cup heavy cream

2 tablespoons butter

Salt and pepper

FOR THE LEMON YOGURT:

7 tablespoons thick plain yogurt

2 tablespoons chopped fresh cilantro

Grated zest of 1 lemon

1 Tuck the herbs into the hollow side of the celery stalk and bind with string to make a bouquet garni.

2 Heat the oil in a large pan. Add the onions, carrots, garlic, and spices, and sauté for 5 minutes, stirring to prevent burning.

3 Add the bouquet garni, lentils, and stock. Bring to a boil. Lower the heat and simmer, covered, for 40 to 45 minutes, stirring occasionally, until the lentils are tender. Discard the bouquet garni.

4 Process until smooth in a blender or food processor; you may need to do this in batches. Return to the clean pan and reheat slowly. Stir in lemon juice, cream, and butter. Season.

5 Make the lemon yogurt: Mix the yogurt with half the cilantro and half the lemon zest. Divide the soup among 4 bowls and add a spoonful of the lemon yogurt to each. Scatter the remaining cilantro and lemon zest over to serve.

Simple Curried Vegetable Broth

PREPARATION: 20 MINUTES

COOKING: 20 TO 30 MINUTES

SERVES 4

1 tablespoon olive oil

1 onion, minced

2 celery stalks, chopped

1 large potato, chopped

2 carrots, chopped

1 parsnip, chopped into large chunks

2 tablespoons mild curry paste or garam masala

1 tablespoon all-purpose flour

4 cups vegetable stock

2 tablespoons heavy cream

Salt and pepper

FOR THE GARNISH:

1 tablespoon butter

1 large onion, thinly sliced

2 tablespoons chopped fresh cilantro

1 Heat the oil in a large pan. Add the vegetables, toss well, and cook for 3 to 4 minutes until light brown.

2 Stir in the curry paste or garam masala and the flour, and stir together well. Pour the stock over and bring to a boil. Lower the heat and simmer, stirring occasionally, for 20 to 30 minutes, until the vegetables are tender.

3 Meanwhile, prepare the garnish: Melt the butter in a skillet. Add the onion and slowly sauté for 7 to 10 minutes until brown.

4 Stir the cream into the soup and adjust the seasoning. Serve immediately, sprinkled with the fried onion and chopped cilantro.

Mushroom-Wonton Soup

PREPARATION: 25 MINUTES, PLUS 30 MINUTES CHILLING
COOKING: 15 MINUTES
SERVES 4

1 cup all-purpose flour, plus extra for dusting

1 teaspoon sugar

2 tablespoons sesame oil

1 teaspoon white wine vinegar

$1^1/_4$ ounces dried shiitake or other dried mushrooms

$^2/_3$ cup boiling water

6 ounces fresh crimini mushrooms

Bunch of scallions, sliced

2 tablespoons soy sauce

5 cups vegetable stock

$^1/_2$ small red chile, thinly sliced

1-inch piece ginger root, grated

2 garlic cloves, thinly sliced

2 tablespoons dry sherry

Peanut oil for brushing

3 ounces Chinese thin egg noodles

3 cups shredded bok choy or spinach

1 Mix flour, sugar, sesame oil, and vinegar with enough warm water to make a firm dough, and knead lightly. Chill for 30 minutes.
2 Soak the dried mushrooms in the boiling water for 10 minutes; drain, reserving the liquid. Place half the mushrooms in a food processor with two-thirds of the crimini mushrooms, half the scallions, and 1 tablespoon of the soy sauce and blend to a paste.
3 On a lightly floured surface, roll out the dough very thinly into a 12-inch square. Trim and cut into sixteen 3-inch squares. Spoon a little mushroom paste into the middle of each. Bring one corner diagonally over the filling and seal the edges to form little triangles.
4 Bring the stock and mushroom liquid to a boil in the bottom of a steamer. Add the remaining mushrooms and the scallions, soy sauce, chile, ginger, garlic, and sherry.
5 Oil a steaming rack and arrange the wontons in a single layer. Cover and steam for 10 minutes. Add the noodles and bok choy or spinach to the soup. Turn the wontons and cook 3 to 5 minutes longer, until tender.
6 Serve the soup and noodles in bowls, topped with the steamed wontons.

Spicy Parsnip Soup

PREPARATION: ABOUT 20 MINUTES

COOKING: ABOUT 30 MINUTES

SERVES 4

1 heaped tablespoon coriander seeds

1 teaspoon each cumin seeds and turmeric

1 dried chile, or ¹/₂ teaspoon red pepper flakes

¹/₄ teaspoon ground fenugreek

2 heaped tablespoons butter

1 onion, chopped

1 large garlic clove, split

2 to 3 large parsnips, cubed

1 tablespoon all-purpose flour

5 cups beef stock

²/₃ cup light cream

Chopped chives or parsley, to garnish

1 Pound the coriander and cumin seeds with the turmeric, chile, and fenugreek in a mortar, or grind them in a spice mill. Put the mixture into a small jar—you will not need it all for this recipe, but can use it up as flavoring for lentils or spinach.

2 Melt the butter in a heavy-bottomed pan. Add the onion, garlic, and parsnips, and cook, covered, over medium heat for 10 minutes. Stir in the flour and 1 tablespoon of the spice mixture. Cook for 2 minutes longer, stirring from time to time. Pour in the stock gradually and bring to a boil. Lower the heat and allow to simmer. When the parsnip is really tender, puree in a blender. Return to the clean pan and dilute to taste with water.

3 Reheat, add the cream, and adjust the seasoning. Serve scattered with chives or parsley. Croutons of bread (page 62) can be served also.

Vegetable Stock

This stock makes an excellent base for any soup. It keeps, covered, in the refrigerator for up to a week or frozen for one month. If you intend to reduce it down for a sauce, don't add any salt.

PREPARATION: 15 MINUTES

COOKING: ABOUT 1¼ HOURS

MAKES ABOUT 3¼ QUARTS

4 pounds mixed vegetables, preferably
   including carrots, onions, celery stalks, and
   tomatoes, coarsely chopped

Large handful fresh parsley, chopped

1 garlic clove, halved (optional)

1 small red chile (optional)

1 bay leaf

1 teaspoon black peppercorns

Salt

1 Put all the ingredients, except the salt, in a large pot. Add 4 quarts cold water and bring to a boil.

2 Lower the heat to a slow simmer and cook, uncovered, for about 1 hour, skimming the surface if necessary.

3 Strain through a fine strainer, discarding the solids. Season to taste with salt.

NOTE: The inclusion of leek and cabbage adds body to the stock, but be sure not to use too much of any one vegetable or it will overpower the others.

Velvety Cauliflower-Cheese Soup

PREPARATION: 15 MINUTES
COOKING: ABOUT 40 MINUTES
SERVES 6

1 large cauliflower 1½ to 2 pounds, broken
    into large florets
Salt and pepper
5 tablespoons butter
1 Spanish or white mild onion, chopped
3 cups 2% milk
3 tablespoons light cream
1 heaping tablespoon all-purpose flour
Chopped fresh parsley, to garnish
FOR THE TOPPINGS:
6 sheets rice paper (about 6 x 8 inches)
1¼ cups finely grated Gruyère cheese
1 tablespoon vegetable oil
2 teaspoons black mustard seeds

1 Preheat the oven to 400°F. Reserve about 1 cup of the cauliflower, then blanch the rest in a pan of boiling salted water for 2 to 3 minutes; drain well.

2 Melt the butter in a pan. Add the onion and sauté for 4 minutes until it is soft but not brown. Add the blanched cauliflower and cook for 2 minutes. Add the milk and 1¼ cups water and bring to a boil. Lower the heat and simmer for 20 minutes until the cauliflower is tender and soft.

3 Meanwhile, make the toppings: Lay 3 sheets of rice paper on each of 2 large baking sheets. Scatter the cheese over evenly. Bake for about 10 minutes until the cheese melts and is light golden; don't let it turn dark brown or the crackers will develop a bitter taste. When cooler, break into large pieces and set aside.

4 Break the reserved cauliflower into tiny florets. Heat the vegetable oil in a small nonstick pan until hot. Add the florets and sauté until light brown. Add the mustard seeds and shake the pan until the seeds pop and release their flavor; take care, some of the seeds may jump out of the pan.

5 In a small bowl, mix the cream and flour to a paste. Add a spoonful of the hot soup and stir well. Stir the mixture back into the soup and cook slowly, stirring, until slightly thicker. Season, then puree in a blender until smooth and creamy.

6 Spoon into warmed soup bowls, sprinkle with stir-fried cauliflower and mustard seeds and the cheesy rice crackers. Garnish with parsley and serve.

Minty Pea and Ham Soup

Mint freshens up this old favorite. This soup needs a quality stock, so a boullion cube just won't do this time.

PREPARATION: 15 MINUTES
COOKING: ABOUT 20 MINUTES
SERVES 4

4 tablespoons butter
About ⅔ cup very thinly sliced leeks
3½ cups frozen peas
1¾ cups finely diced cooked ham from
    the bone
2 quarts good-quality, preferably homemade,
    chicken or vegetable stock (see page 17)
1 tablespoon shredded fresh mint, plus a few
    sprigs for garnish
Salt and pepper

1 Melt the butter in a pan. Add the leeks and sauté slowly for 3 to 4 minutes. Add the peas and ham and toss together.

2 Add the stock and bring to a boil. Lower the heat and simmer for 15 minutes. Season to taste.

3 Puree half the soup in a blender until very smooth; return to the pan with the remaining soup. Mix well, then add the mint and heat through.

4 Spoon some soup into each of 4 warmed bowls and garnish with mint sprigs.

Along with potatoes and onions, tomatoes have become one of the most ubiquitous vegetables—in the stores all year round and relatively inexpensive. Although a native of South America, this bright red member of the nightshade family didn't gain popularity in the United States until the turn of the century. It is technically a fruit, but has been classified as a vegetable for trade purposes. Unfortunately, as with any food made so readily available, quality and flavor seem to have been sacrificed for convenience. It is therefore worth trying some of the new varieties to find the most delicious specimens. As with most "vegetable fruits," flavor is largely a function of ripeness, and the best indication of ripeness is a deep (usually red) color.

Tomatoes should be kept at room temperature—the low temperatures of the refrigerator mask any flavor. Perfectly ripe specimens will keep for a day or two; underripe ones for up to a week. If they've gone beyond perfectly ripe to become very soft and squishy, don't discard them. They will still be fine cooked in a sauce.

Unless cooking tomatoes whole or halved (as in stuffing), or in a dish to be strained or pureed, it is usually best to remove the skins, as they otherwise become stringy. Put the tomatoes in a bowl, pour boiling water over, and let stand for 20 seconds. Drain and refresh with cold water. The skins should then come away easily.

Tomatoes

Old-Fashioned Tomato Sauce

A classic tomato sauce is easy enough to buy, but the taste of a home-cooked version is so much better. We've kept this sauce simple, so nothing competes with the flavor of the tomatoes—but if you want to zip it up, add your own favorite flavorings. This makes about 3 cups.

1 Skin and seed 3 pounds ripe tomatoes (see above), then roughly chop the flesh. Heat 3 tablespoons olive oil in a heavy-bottomed pan. Add 1 small chopped onion and 1 finely chopped garlic clove and cook over low heat for 4 to 5 minutes until soft but not brown.

2 Add the tomatoes and cook, covered, over medium heat for 25 to 30 minutes, stirring often. Toward the end, add 1 tablespoon fresh or frozen oregano (or 1 teaspoon dried). The sauce is ready when the tomatoes have broken down to produce a thick consistency. Season to taste. If it needs a little more sweetness, stir in up to $^1/_2$ teaspoon sugar.

3 Pour into a covered glass or plastic container and store in the refrigerator. Use within 3 or 4 days.

4 For a smoother consistency, to serve with spaghetti, for example, strain the finished sauce; just don't skin the tomatoes in Step 1. Do seed them, however, or the flavor of the sauce will be diluted.

Jerusalem Artichoke Soup

Jerusalem artichokes, also called sunchokes, are among the unsung heroes of the vegetable world and make delicious soups. This soup can be prepared ahead, or frozen at the end of Step 3.

PREPARATION: 25 MINUTES
COOKING: 50 MINUTES
SERVES 8
2 tablespoons butter
2 onions, sliced
1³/₄ pounds Jerusalem artichokes
2¹/₂ cups vegetable stock or potato cooking water
Salt and white pepper
Pinch of sugar
2¹/₂ cups milk
2 tablespoons light cream, to finish
Croutons (see page 62), to serve

1 Melt the butter in a large heavy pan. Add the onions, cover, and let them sweat for 5 minutes until soft but not brown.
2 Peel and slice the Jerusalem artichokes, then add them to the softened onions and sauté for about 15 minutes, or until they are just tender.
3 Pour in the vegetable stock or potato cooking water and season with salt, white pepper, and the sugar. Bring to a boil. Lower the heat and simmer for about 20 minutes, until the Jerusalem artichokes are soft.
4 In a blender or food processor, puree the soup in batches. Pour the puree back into the clean pan and stir in the milk.
5 Heat the soup slowly to just below a boil. Stir in the cream.
6 Serve with croutons.

Chilled Beet Soup with Horseradish Cream

This brightly colored soup tastes just as vivid as it looks, and couldn't be easier to make. Use a blender rather than a food processor for a smoother finish.

PREPARATION: 15 MINUTES
SERVES 4
1 orange
12 ounces cooked beets, chopped
2 cups vegetable stock (see page 17)
1 cup thick plain yogurt
Salt and pepper
1 tablespoon prepared horseradish
Fresh mint sprigs, to garnish
Good crusty bread, to serve

1 Using a zester, remove the zest from half the orange, or thinly pare off the zest with a potato peeler and shred it finely. Place in a cup with just enough boiling water to cover and leave to stand for at least 10 minutes to soften. Finely grate the remaining zest and squeeze the juice from the orange.
2 In a blender, combine the beet and vegetable stock and blend until smooth. Blend in half the yogurt and season to taste. Chill until ready to serve.
3 Add the horseradish to the remaining yogurt. Pour the chilled soup into 4 serving bowls. Add a spoonful of the horseradish mixture to each. Drain and pat dry the softened orange zest and scatter over the cream. Garnish with the mint sprigs and serve with some good crusty bread.

Chickpea and Tomato Broth

Serve with a green salad as an appetizer or light lunch.

PREPARATION: 10 MINUTES

COOKING: 20 TO 25 MINUTES

SERVES 4

1 tablespoon sunflower oil

1 onion, chopped

$3^1/_2$ cups diced baking potatoes ($^1/_2$-inch cubes)

$^1/_2$ to 1 tablespoon curry paste or powder

3 cups vegetable stock

1 (14-ounce) can tomatoes

1 (15-ounce) can chickpeas, drained

1 heaping cup frozen peas

Squeeze of lemon juice

Salt and pepper

TO SERVE:

Warm naan bread

Plain yogurt

1 Heat the oil in a large heavy-bottomed pan. Add the onion and potatoes, and sauté, stirring, for 3 to 4 minutes.

2 Stir in the curry paste or powder and the stock and bring to a boil. Lower the heat and simmer for 10 to 15 minutes.

3 Add the tomatoes with their liquid, the chickpeas, and the peas. Simmer for 5 minutes longer.

4 Season with a little lemon juice and salt and pepper to taste. Ladle into bowls and serve with naan bread and some yogurt in a separate bowl.

Vegetables make the best of appetizers and light meals, providing delicious flavors and intriguing textures to tease the palate, while staying light and healthy—packed full of nutrients. Try them in combination with traditional cheeses, in fluffy omelets and soufflés, or crisp tartlets. Alternatively, deliver all their crunch in piquant salads.

Making Overtures

Appetizers, Snacks, and Light Meals

Feta and Anchovy Stuffed Peppers

The delicious roasted sweetness and the color of the red bell peppers contrast brilliantly with the sharpness of the crumbly white cheese. Instead of red peppers you can also use yellow or orange peppers. As a change from feta, you could use another crumbly cheese, such as a sharp goat cheese.

You can roast the peppers up to a day ahead, cover, and chill. Remove from the refrigerator 30 minutes before serving.

PREPARATION: 15 MINUTES
BAKING: 25 TO 30 MINUTES
SERVES 6
3 red bell peppers
1¹/₂ (2 ounce) cans anchovies, drained
1 garlic clove, minced
¹/₂ pound cherry tomatoes, quartered
2 tablespoons olive oil
2 teaspoons balsamic vinegar
Salt and pepper
5 ounces feta cheese
Fresh basil leaves, shredded

1 Preheat the oven to 375°F. Quarter and seed the peppers. Put them in a single layer in a roasting pan, skin-side down. Cut the anchovies into 24 strips.
2 Mix together the garlic, tomatoes, oil, vinegar, and salt and pepper to taste. Spoon a little of this mixture into the cavity of each pepper. Arrange 2 anchovy strips crossed on each. Bake for 25 to 30 minutes until the peppers are tender. Leave to cool.

3 Slice the feta thinly, then break it into pieces. Put 2 pepper pieces on each plate and drizzle the pan juices over. Sprinkle with the crumbled feta and shredded basil.

New Vegetables à la Grecque

For variety, use snow peas or sugar snap peas instead of fava beans.

PREPARATION: 15 MINUTES
COOKING: 25 MINUTES
SERVES 4
5 tablespoons olive oil
1 large garlic clove, crushed
3 baby eggplants or 1 small eggplant, finely diced
1 red or yellow onion, thinly sliced
1 large tomato, skinned and chopped
3 tablespoons sun-dried tomato paste
2 tablespoons red wine vinegar
Salt and pepper
1 pound baby new potatoes, scrubbed and halved
12 ounces baby carrots, halved
3 cups shelled fava beans
4 ounces young asparagus stalks
TO SERVE:
¹/₄ cup ripe olives
1 tablespoon capers
Flat-leaf parsley leaves
Crusty bread, to serve

1 Heat the olive oil in a skillet. Add the garlic, eggplant, and onion, and cook over medium heat until very soft, about 10 minutes.

2 Transfer the mixture to a very large bowl and stir in the chopped tomato and sun-dried tomato paste. Add the red wine vinegar and season to taste with salt and pepper; set aside.
3 Cook the potatoes and carrots in a pan of lightly salted boiling water for about 15 minutes, until tender; drain well. Meanwhile, steam the fava beans and asparagus for about 5 minutes, until just tender.
4 While the vegetables are still hot, add them to the eggplant mixture. Stir well to coat and leave to cool for about 5 minutes before serving so they absorb the flavors of the sauce.
5 Serve sprinkled with ripe olives, capers, and parsley leaves, accompanied by crusty bread.

Baked Goat Cheese Bundles with Sweet-and-Sour Leeks

This dish looks spectacular, but, surprisingly, most of the ingredients are simple pantry basics. The goat cheese bundles and the beet dressing can be prepared the day before and kept covered in the refrigerator. The tomato garnish can be made up to 2 hours in advance.

PREPARATION: 40 MINUTES

BAKING: 5 MINUTES

SERVES 4

8 sheets phyllo pastry dough, each about
   13 x 7 inches

5 tablespoons butter, melted

6 ounces soft, rindless goat cheese

1/2 cup roughly chopped mixed shelled
   hazelnuts and pistachio nuts

Salt and pepper

FOR THE BEET DRESSING:

1/3 cup chopped cooked beet

1/4 teaspoon Dijon mustard

1 tablespoon red-wine vinegar

1/2 teaspoon sugar

4 tablespoons olive oil

FOR THE SWEET-AND-SOUR LEEKS:

4 tablespoons olive oil

2 garlic cloves, crushed

2 teaspoons sugar

2 1/4 pounds leeks, trimmed, cleaned, cut
   in half lengthwise and then into chunks

Juice of 1 lemon

FOR THE TOMATO GARNISH:

1 tomato

2 tablespoons olive oil

2 teaspoons mixed fresh herbs, such as
   flat-leafed parsley, thyme, and oregano

1 Working quickly before the dough dries and keeping all but the sheet you are working on under a damp dish towel, place a sheet of phyllo on a flat surface and brush it all over with a little of the melted butter. Place the second sheet on top and cut in half to make 2 squares. Brush one with a little more butter and place the other stack on top at an angle to create an 8-pointed star. Butter the top layer of dough; repeat to make 4 stacked dough stars.

2 Cut the goat cheese into 4 equal pieces and shape each piece into a ball. Place a cheese ball in the middle of each phyllo star. Sprinkle the nuts over and season. Bring together the corners of each star and twist to make a bundle. Place on a cookie sheet and brush with the remaining butter. Chill until required.

3 Preheat the oven to 400°F. To make the beet dressing, place all the ingredients in a food processor with 3 tablespoons water and blend until smooth; set aside until required.

4 To make the sweet-and-sour leeks, heat the oil in a large pan. Add the garlic and sugar, and stir until the sugar caramelizes. Add the leeks and sprinkle with the lemon juice. Cover and simmer for 4 to 5 minutes.

5 Meanwhile, bake the phyllo bundles for 5 minutes until golden and crisp at the edges.

6 To make the tomato garnish, first cut the tomato into quarters and scoop out the seeds. Then run a sharp knife underneath the flesh of the each tomato quarter to remove the skin. Cut each quarter into 4 strips and toss in the oil and herbs.

7 To assemble, place a small mound of the leeks in the middle of each plate and place a goat cheese bundle on top. Spoon around the beet dressing and decorate each plate with the tomato garnish.

Feta and Herb Briouats

"Briouat" is the Moroccan name for a stuffed pastry made with warka, the local wafer-thin pastry dough. However, this version uses phyllo dough, available from supermarkets, instead.

PREPARATION: 60 MINUTES

COOKING: 20 TO 25 MINUTES

MAKES 24

4 tablespoons butter or 2 to 3 tablespoons
    olive oil

3 onions, halved and thinly sliced

1 teaspoon salt

$^1/_2$ teaspoon ground cinnamon

5 eggs, beaten

2 tablespoons coarsely chopped flat-leaf
    parsley

$1^1/_2$ tablespoons coarsely chopped fresh
    cilantro

3 ounces feta cheese, diced

Salt and pepper

FOR THE PASTRY:

12 sheets phyllo pastry dough, defrosted
    if frozen

4 tablespoons melted butter, or 4 tablespoons
    olive oil

FOR THE RED BELL PEPPER AND
TOMATO SAUCE:

1 (14 ounce) jar roasted red bell peppers

1 (14 ounce) jar diced tomatoes

Pinch of saffron strands, softened in a little
    boiling water

1 tablespoon honey

Salt and pepper

2 garlic cloves, crushed

Squeeze of lemon juice

1 Melt about half the butter or heat half the olive oil in a skillet over medium heat. Stir in the thinly sliced onions and sprinkle with the salt. Cook for a few minutes, stirring. Cover the pan and cook, stirring occasionally, until the onions are soft but not colored.

2 Stir in the ground cinnamon, beaten eggs, and remaining butter or olive oil. Keep over low heat for 2 to 3 minutes until the eggs are thick but still moist (like scrambled eggs). Stir in the chopped herbs and the feta; season to taste. Transfer to a bowl and leave to cool.

3 To make the red bell pepper and tomato sauce, first drain the peppers. Then put them in a blender or food processor with the tomatoes, saffron, honey, and salt and pepper to taste. Blend this mixture to a puree. Pour into a pan, add the garlic, and simmer for 30 minutes, until reduced by about half and thick.

4 Meanwhile, preheat the oven to 350°F. Working as quickly as you can with one sheet of phyllo pastry dough (keep the rest of them under a damp dish towel so they don't dry out), brush half of one side down the length with the melted butter or olive oil. Fold this over to make a long strip; paint the folded surface with more butter or oil. Cut the sheet in half across its width.

5 Place a good teaspoon of the feta mixture on the bottom of each half of buttered dough. Fold over the edges, brush the surface of the dough with more melted butter or oil, and roll it up like a plump egg roll. Brush with more melted butter or oil and place on a greased cookie sheet, seam-side down. Repeat to make 24 pastries.

6 Bake the pastries for 20 to 25 minutes until golden. Finish the sauce by seasoning to taste with the lemon juice and more salt and pepper if necessary. Serve it with the hot briouats.

Eggplant and Mozzarella Stacks

These Mediterranean towers will bring sunshine flavors to your table at any time of year. Serve with garlic bread. You can make this dish ahead; make the stacks up to the end of Step 2, then cover and chill for up to 24 hours. Make the sauce, cover, and chill for up to 2 days.

PREPARATION: 25 MINUTES

BAKING: 15 TO 20 MINUTES

SERVES 6

1 medium eggplant

2 tablespoons olive oil, plus more for the dish

5 ounces fresh mozzarella cheese, drained

6 slices prosciutto

Handful basil leaves, torn, to serve

FOR THE SAUCE:

1 (15 ounce) can crushed tomatoes and 2 teaspoons tomato paste

2 tablespoons extra-virgin olive oil

1 garlic clove, chopped

1 Preheat the oven to 400°F and preheat the broiler. Cut 12 eggplant slices about ¹/₂ inch thick. Arrange these in the broiler pan in one layer and brush with half the olive oil. Broil for 3 to 4 minutes until well colored. Turn over, brush, and broil again; leave to cool.

2 Cut the mozzarella cheese into 6 slices. Sandwich each between 2 eggplant slices. Put the "sandwiches" in a greased shallow baking dish and crumple the prosciutto on top. Bake for 12 to 15 minutes, until the cheese melts.

3 While they are baking, make the sauce. Put all the ingredients in a pan and simmer briefly (or until slightly thickened, if using canned tomatoes). Spoon a little sauce on each plate, put the stacks on top, and scatter with basil. Serve while still hot.

Tomato Stacks with Herb and Onion Salsa

PREPARATION: ABOUT 25 MINUTES
SERVES 4

3 ounces mixed salad greens
1 large red onion, minced
6 tablespoons finely chopped flat-leafed parsley
6 tablespoons finely chopped cilantro leaves
4 large ripe tomatoes
FOR THE VINAIGRETTE:
$^2/_3$ cup extra-virgin olive oil
Juice of 1 large lime, or 2 tablespoons fresh lemon juice
2 garlic cloves, finely chopped
1 teaspoon Dijon mustard
Salt and pepper
Pinch red pepper flakes
FOR THE GARNISH:
Ripe olives
Sprigs basil, cilantro, and flat-leafed parsley

1 First make the vinaigrette. In a small bowl, whisk together the oil, citrus juice, chopped garlic, and mustard. Season with plenty of salt, pepper, and red pepper flakes; set aside.
2 Tear half the salad leaves into small pieces and put in a bowl. Stir in the onion, parsley, and cilantro. Spoon the vinaigrette over, toss, cover with plastic wrap, and chill until required.
3 Cut a thin slice off the bottom of each tomato so it will stand up when stacked. Cut each tomato horizontally into 5 even slices; reassemble each tomato as you do, so you know which slices belong to which tomato.
4 Stir the red-onion salsa so it is well mixed. Put the bottom slice of one tomato on a chilled salad plate. Spoon a little salsa over and season with salt and pepper. Place the second slice on top. Repeat the layers to complete the stacks; repeat with the remaining 3 tomatoes.
5 Arrange a few olives, the rest of the salad leaves, and fresh herb sprigs around each plate. Drizzle any remaining salsa over the salad. Garnish each tomato with parsley leaves and an olive. Serve immediately.

Vegetable Patties with Spicy Tomato Chutney

These vegetarian patties are made from a base of sweet potato, with the addition of grated zucchini and grated carrots.

PREPARATION: 15 MINUTES, PLUS 30 MINUTES STANDING
COOKING: ABOUT 30 MINUTES
SERVES 4

12 ounces zucchini
Salt and pepper
1$^1/_4$ pounds sweet potatoes
3 to 4 carrots (about 8 ounces)
1 green chile
1 scallion
2 tablespoons plain yogurt
Flour for dusting
Vegetable oil for frying
FOR THE SPICY TOMATO CHUTNEY:
4 tomatoes
1 to 2 red chiles
2 tablespoons chopped fresh mint
1 tablespoon cider vinegar
Pinch sea salt

1 First make the chutney. Roughly chop the tomatoes and mince the chiles. Mix both with the mint, vinegar, and salt; set aside until ready to serve.
2 To make the patties, first grate the zucchini and sprinkle them with salt; set aside for 30 minutes to draw out some of the watery juices. Meanwhile, boil the sweet potatoes until tender; drain and mash them. Grate the carrots. Seed and chop the chile. Slice the scallion. Rinse the zucchini, drain well, and pat dry.
3 Mix the vegetables, yogurt, and salt and pepper in a bowl. With floured hands, shape the mixture into 8 patties.
4 Heat a shallow layer of oil in a heavy-bottomed skillet. Add the patties and fry for 4 minutes on each side.
5 Serve the patties with the spicy chutney.

31

Honeyed Carrot and Fig Couscous

This Persian-style dish can be made using bulgur instead of couscous, if you prefer. For an extra tangy flavor, cook the carrots in fresh fruit or vegetable juice.

PREPARATION: 10 MINUTES, PLUS STANDING
COOKING: 20 MINUTES
SERVES 4

4 tablespoons honey

Finely grated zest and juice of 1 lemon

3^3/$_4$ cups vegetable stock

1 pound baby carrots, trimmed

2 cups couscous

1 teaspoon garlic paste

1 pomegranate

3 ripe figs, quartered

2 tablespoons chopped fresh flat-leaf parsley

1 tablespoon chopped fresh mint

Salt and pepper

1 Place the honey and lemon zest and juice in a large shallow pan with 1^1/$_4$ cups of the stock. Stir and bring to a boil. Add the carrots and simmer over very low heat for 10 minutes. Return to a boil and boil for 8 minutes until the liquid is thick and caramelized.

2 Meanwhile, place the couscous in a shallow dish. Mix the remaining vegetable stock and garlic paste together and pour over the couscous to cover. Leave to stand for 10 minutes until all the liquid has been absorbed.

3 Scoop the seeds and pulp from the pomegranate. Fluff up the couscous and toss with the pomegranate, figs, and herbs. Season and serve with the carrots and remaining syrup.

Goat Cheese and Polenta with Mushrooms

This glamorous first course also makes a quick supper dish. Use instant polenta, because it cooks so quickly, and a firm goat cheese—look for chèvre logs. Both are available from most supermarkets.

PREPARATION: 5 MINUTES
COOKING: 10 MINUTES
SERVES 4

2 cups dry white wine

1 teaspoon salt

6 tablespoons butter, cut into pieces

1 cup instant polenta

6 ounces firm goat cheese, rind removed, cubed

3 tablespoons olive oil

3 cups mixed wild and crimini mushrooms, which have
     been trimmed and cut into pieces

10 ounces young leaf spinach

^{1}/$_2$ cup grated cheddar cheese

4 scallions, finely shredded, to garnish

1 Put the wine in a large pan with 2 cups water and bring to a boil. Stir in the salt and butter, stirring until the butter melts. Add the polenta in a steady stream, whisking constantly until cooked (usually about 2 minutes, but check the directions on the package). Remove from the heat and stir in the goat cheese; the polenta should be soft and spoonable.

2 In a pan, heat 1 tablespoon of the oil. Add the mushrooms and sauté for 2 minutes; remove and set aside. Sauté the spinach in 2 batches, each in 1 tablespoon of olive oil, until just wilted—no longer than 1 minute.

3 Spoon the goat-cheese polenta into wide serving bowls and pile up the spinach and mushrooms in the middle. Scatter the grated cheddar cheese and shredded scallions over. Serve immediately.

Warm Salad of Roasted Eggplant and Tomatoes with Cannellini Beans

PREPARATION: 30 MINUTES

ROASTING: ABOUT 1 1/2 HOURS

SERVES 6 AS AN APPETIZER OR 4 AS A SNACK

1 large or 2 small eggplants, about 12 ounces in total weight

2 pounds tomatoes

1/2 garlic bulb, halved vertically, top trimmed but cloves left unseparated

2 red chiles

2 teaspoons honey

6 tablespoons olive oil

Salt and pepper

1 cup dried cannellini beans, cooked, or 1 (14 ounce) can

Generous pinch saffron threads

2 teaspoons red wine vinegar

1 heaped tablespoon minced fresh parsley

1 Preheat the oven to 325°F. Cut the eggplant into 2-inch thick slices; quarter the slices. Cut a cone from the top of each tomato to remove the core. Cut the tomatoes in half, or quarter them if large.

2 Arrange the eggplant pieces, tomatoes, garlic, and chiles in a roasting pan. Drizzle the honey and olive oil over, and season with salt and pepper. Roast for 1 1/2 hours, basting occasionally.

3 Remove and discard the chiles. Squeeze the garlic from its skin back into the vegetables. Spoon the vegetables into a serving dish, leaving the juices in the pan. Plunge the cannellini beans into boiling water until hot; drain and pat dry. Add the beans to the vegetables and stir well.

4 Grind the saffron in a mortar, then blend with 2 teaspoons boiling water. Add to the roasting pan with the vinegar and stir until blended. Season to taste. Pour over the vegetables and beans. Scatter the parsley over and serve warm.

Vegetable Omelet

PREPARATION: 15 MINUTES
COOKING: 15 TO 20 MINUTES
SERVES 4

4 tablespoons olive oil

1 onion, sliced

1 garlic clove, minced

1 eggplant, cut into chunks

2 zucchini, cut into chunks

2 tomatoes, cut into wedges

Salt and pepper

6 eggs

$^1/_2$ teaspoon dried oregano

Handful fresh basil leaves (optional)

Green salad, to serve

1 Heat the oil in a skillet with a flameproof handle. Add the onion and cook until soft. Add the garlic, eggplant, and zucchini chunks, and cook for 5 to 8 minutes until soft and light brown. Add the tomato wedges and season with salt and pepper.

2 Meanwhile, beat the eggs in a bowl. Stir in the dried oregano and season. Preheat the broiler.

3 Pour the beaten eggs over the vegetables and cook for 5 to 8 minutes until the bottom starts to brown and the eggs look softly set.

4 Slide the omelet under the broiler and broil until the top looks puffed and golden.

5 Tear the basil leaves over, if using. Cut into wedges and serve with a green salad.

Asparagus is now available all year round, but it is best from February through June, when it is in season in various parts of the country.

When shopping, look for firm, unwrinkled stalks, and avoid any with wet cut ends because that can mean they have been standing in water to try to refresh them. Also check that packed bunches don't hide inferior or much smaller or mis-shapen stalks in their centers. When you buy loose stalks, choose ones of roughly the same thickness so they will all cook at the same rate.

You can keep your asparagus stalks fresh at home by standing them in water, but it is much better to use them quickly.

To prepare asparagus, remove the woody stalks from a point just above where it starts to feel softer to the touch. All but the youngest and most tender stalks are also improved by lightly peeling off the stringy outer skins.

Asparagus is usually steamed or boiled; traditional asparagus pots allow the stalks to be boiled while the tips steam more gently at the top. Yet it has become fashionable to roast or grill asparagus stalks briefly after painting the stalks very lightly with olive oil or melted butter.

Asparagus

Asparagus with Lime and Cilantro Butter

This citrus butter gives a superb zesty kick to any simple steamed vegetable, noodles, or even baked potatoes. It will keep in the refrigerator for 2 weeks and in the freezer for 1 month.

1 To make the lime and cilantro butter: first place 4 tablespoons soft butter in a bowl with the grated zest and juice of 1 lime and 2 tablespoons chopped fresh cilantro, then beat together until smooth. Spoon onto waxed paper and roll up to form a log shape. Twist the ends of the paper to seal and place in the refrigerator until firm.

2 Trim 2 pounds fresh young asparagus and peel as appropriate (see introduction). Steam for 10 to 15 minutes, until just tender. Drain well and pat dry.

3 Cut the chilled log of flavored butter into slices and serve with the hot asparagus.

Asparagus and Soft Egg Tartlets

Served with a green salad, this makes a great first course or light lunch.

PREPARATION: 20 MINUTES, PLUS 30
MINUTES CHILLING
BAKING: 25 TO 30 MINUTES
MAKES 4
FOR THE PASTRY DOUGH:
2/3 cup all-purpose flour
4 tablespoons butter, cut into small pieces
1 small egg
FOR THE FILLING:
4 ounces thin asparagus stalks
Salt and pepper
4 eggs
2 tablespoons light cream
1 tablespoon finely grated Parmesan or sharp
   cheddar cheese
Freshly grated nutmeg

1 To make the dough, place the flour in a food processor. Add the butter and process until the mixture resembles fine crumbs. Add the egg and work briefly to form a dough. Place the dough on a lightly floured surface and knead briefly. Wrap in plastic wrap and chill for at least 30 minutes.

2 Preheat the oven to 400°F. Cut the asparagus into 2-inch pieces. Bring a large pan of salted water to a boil. Add the asparagus and cook for 5 minutes; drain and cool quickly in cold water.

3 Divide the dough into 4 equal pieces. Roll out each piece and use to line four 4-inch tartlet pans. Trim off the excess dough with a sharp knife. Set the pans on a cookie sheet. Line each dough shell with a circle of foil and half fill with baking beans or uncooked rice. Bake for 12 to 15 minutes. Remove the paper and beans and bake for 3 to 4 minutes longer, until the pastry is crisp and light golden.

4 Divide the asparagus among the tartlets, then break an egg into each. Drizzle the cream over and sprinkle with the grated cheese, a little nutmeg, and salt and pepper. Return to the oven for 5 to 8 minutes, until the egg is just set and the top lightly browned.

5 Serve warm or cold.

Roasted Asparagus with Poached Eggs

PREPARATION: 10 MINUTES
COOKING: 20 TO 25 MINUTES
SERVES 6
1 pound thin asparagus stalks
2 tablespoons butter
1 cup fresh white breadcrumbs
Salt and pepper
Grated zest of 1 lemon
3 tablespoons minced fresh parsley
Olive oil for brushing and drizzling
2/3 cup white wine vinegar
6 very fresh eggs
Parmesan shavings, to serve

1 There is no need to peel the asparagus, but if it is thick, snap off any woody stalks at the point where they break easily.

2 Preheat the oven to 400°F. Melt the butter in a pan. Add the breadcrumbs and fry, stirring often, until crisp; remove from the heat. Season and stir in lemon zest and parsley.

3 Lay the asparagus on a greased cookie sheet and brush them with oil. Roast for 12 to 15 minutes.

4 Meanwhile, half fill a saucepan with water. Add the vinegar and bring to a boil. Crack in the eggs from a height of about 4 inches (this gives them a good round shape). Simmer for 3 to 4 minutes, until the white is firm. Using a slotted spoon, transfer the eggs to a bowl of warm water (they will keep warm this way for up to 30 minutes).

5 Arrange the asparagus on plates. Drizzle with more oil and scatter the Parmesan shavings over. Spoon the eggs on top and sprinkle with the crumbs. Season with coarse sea salt and black pepper.

Things on Toast

SPICY AVOCADO AND
CILANTRO ON CORN BREAD TOAST

SERVES 4

Toast 4 thick slices of corn bread (or white bread) on both sides. Splash with extra-virgin olive oil and sprinkle with sea salt. Scoop teaspoons of flesh from 2 avocados and arrange them on the toasts. Squeeze some fresh lemon or lime juice over. Add a splash of hot pepper sauce, more salt and olive oil, pepper, and a handful of torn cilantro leaves.

ROASTED HAM AND
MUSHROOM TOAST

SERVES 4

Preheat the oven to 425°F. Mix 4 tablespoons olive oil with 1 minced garlic clove. Arrange 4 large flat mushrooms, stems removed, in a roasting pan and brush with a little of this garlic oil. Top each with a slice of ham and a quarter of a seeded red bell pepper, and brush with a little more garlic oil. Sprinkle with some salt and pepper. Roast for about 15 minutes, until the mushrooms are just starting to soften.

Meanwhile, brush 4 large thick slices of white bread on both sides with the remaining garlic oil. Put on a cookie sheet and bake for 15 minutes. Remove the mushrooms from the oven and top each with a thin slice of Stilton or other blue cheese. Return to the oven for 5 minutes longer.

To serve, put a stuffed mushroom on each piece of toast and drizzle with the juices from the roasting pan.

MUSHROOMS WITH TRUFFLE OIL
ON ITALIAN COUNTRY TOAST

SERVES 4

Thickly slice 6 large mushrooms and toss with about 10 wild mushrooms or soaked and dried porcini slices. In a skillet, heat a little olive oil. Add a chopped garlic clove and the mushrooms, and sauté for 5 to 6 minutes. Stir in 4 table-spoons crème fraîche or sour cream and a pinch of cayenne. Under a medium-hot broiler, toast 4 slices of Italian country-style bread on both sides. Pile the mushroom mixture on top and drizzle a little truffle oil over.

ROASTED VINE TOMATOES
AND ONIONS WITH CHEDDAR

SERVES 4

Preheat the oven to 425°F. Heat 2 tablespoons olive oil in a skillet with a flameproof handle. Add 8 to 12 peeled baby pickling onions, sprinkle with 2 teaspoons sugar, and fry for about 5 minutes until tinged golden brown. Add 1¹/₂ tablespoons white wine vinegar and cook for 4 to 5 minutes, until reduced.

Add 8 ounces baby vine tomatoes on their stems to the pan. Transfer the pan to the oven and roast for 8 minutes.

Meanwhile, preheat the broiler to high. Toast 4 thick slices of white bread on both sides; place on a cookie sheet. Sprinkle with olive oil and salt and pepper. Top with the onion and tomato mixture, and drizzle with any juices left in the pan. Sprinkle with basil leaves and cheddar shavings, and season again. Place under the hot broiler until the cheese melts.

Garlicky Mushroom Toasts

In the fall, you may find wild mushrooms, such as chanterelles and porcini, in the stores. Add just a few, and the crimini mushrooms will take on a lovely wild flavor.

PREPARATION: 10 MINUTES

COOKING: 15 MINUTES

SERVES 6

1 tablespoon olive oil

2 garlic cloves, crushed

$6^1/_2$ cups sliced mixed mushrooms, such as
    crimini and oyster

3 tablespoons Marsala, Madeira, or sweet sherry

$1^1/_4$ cups heavy cream

Salt and pepper

FOR THE TOASTS:

3 chunks ciabatta bread

4 tablespoons butter, softened

4 tablespoons chopped fresh parsley, plus
    more to garnish

1 To make the toasts, first heat the broiler, then split each ciabatta chunk in half and broil on the crust sides. Mix the butter and parsley and spread this over the cut sides of the ciabatta.

2 To cook the mushrooms, first heat the oil in a large skillet, then add the garlic and mushrooms and sauté over fairly high heat for 6 to 7 minutes, turning occasionally; cook until the liquid evaporates.

3 Pour the wine into the pan and let it bubble for a few minutes. Stir in the cream and season with salt and pepper.

4 Toast the cut side of the ciabatta until the butter melts and the bread is golden. Put on plates and spoon the mushrooms over, season with black pepper and garnish with more chopped parsley to serve.

Goat Cheese and Olive Toasts

PREPARATION: 10 MINUTES

BAKING: 8 MINUTES

MAKES 20

10 thin slices white bread, crusts removed

1 tablespoon green olive paste

1 tablespoon black olive paste

1 tablespoon sun-dried tomato paste

8 ounces soft, rindless goat cheese

2 tablespoons chopped fresh parsley

FOR THE BASIL DRESSING:

3 tablespoons olive oil

1 tablespoon balsamic vinegar

1 tablespoon minced fresh basil

Salt and pepper

1 Preheat the oven to 400°F. Spread each slice of bread with one of the olive pastes or the sun-dried tomato paste. Spread each of them with a little of the cheese; warming the cheese for a few seconds in a microwave makes it much easier to spread. Roll each slice up tightly, secure with 2 wooden toothpicks, and arrange, spaced well apart, on a cookie sheet.

2 To make the basil dressing, whisk the oil, vinegar, and basil together well until emulsified. Season with salt and pepper to taste.

3 Brush the toasts with the dressing and sprinkle the parsley over. Toast in the oven for 8 minutes until crisp and golden.

4 Remove the toothpicks and cut each toast into 2 equal pieces. Arrange on a serving plate and serve warm or at room temperature.

Potato Cakes with Chard and Hollandaise

The potato cakes and hollandaise sauce can be made a day in advance, and the dish assembled in minutes.

PREPARATION: 30 MINUTES
COOKING: 15 MINUTES
SERVES 4

Heaping 1 cup baking potatoes cut into large chunks

3 tablespoons crème fraîche or sour cream

3 eggs, separated

$1/4$ cup grated Parmesan cheese

Salt and pepper

1 tablespoon olive oil

FOR THE HOLLANDAISE:

2 large egg yolks

1 tablespoon white wine vinegar

2 tablespoons lemon juice

$3/4$ cup ($1^1/2$ sticks) butter, melted

1 teaspoon whole grain mustard

FOR THE TOPPING:

4 tablespoons butter

3 cups shredded chard

2 heaping cups sliced wild mushrooms such as shiitake, chanterelles, and oyster

8 scallions, shredded

$1/4$ teaspoon grated nutmeg

Salt and pepper

1 Cook the potatoes in boiling, salted water for 6 to 8 minutes until just tender; drain and leave to cool.
2 To make the hollandaise, first place the egg yolks and a pinch of salt in a food processor and process. In a pan, bring the vinegar and lemon juice just to a boil. With the motor still running, gradually add the vinegar and lemon juice to the egg yolks. Slowly pour in the melted butter and process until thick. Transfer to a bowl and stir in the mustard. Place the bowl in a pan of hot water to keep warm.

3 Coarsely grate the potatoes. Stir in the crème fraîche or sour cream, egg yolks, Parmesan, and seasoning to taste.
4 In a large bowl, whisk the egg whites until they form soft peaks. Using a metal spoon, beat a little egg white into the potato mixture to loosen it, then fold in the rest.
5 Preheat the broiler to medium. Heat the oil in a large non-stick skillet. Lightly oil 4 round biscuit cutters, $3^1/2$ inches across and $1^1/4$ inches deep. Place the cutters in the pan and fill each three-quarters full with potato mixture. Fry for 1 minute until the bottoms are cooked. Place pan under the broiler and broil for a minute until the tops are golden and set; keep warm.
6 To make the topping, first melt the butter in a large skillet, then add the chard, mushrooms, scallions, and nutmeg and cook for 1 to 2 minutes; season to taste.
7 Remove the cutters from the potato cakes and transfer the cakes to plates. Spoon the vegetables on top and drizzle the sauce over.

Tricolor Muffins

This snack is great served warm.

PREPARATION: 10 MINUTES
COOKING: ABOUT 15 MINUTES
MAKES 4

4 English muffins

1 eggplant, thickly cut into 4 slices

2 tablespoons garlic-flavored oil

1 large beefsteak tomato, thickly cut into 4 slices

4 tablespoons crème fraîche or sour cream

4 teaspoons pesto sauce

Handful arugula or watercress

1 Split the muffins in half and lightly toast them.
2 Fry the eggplant slices in the garlic-flavored oil until crisp and blackened.
3 Place a slice of eggplant on each muffin bottom, followed by a thick slice of tomato and a spoonful of crème fraîche or sour cream. Spoon the pesto sauce over and finish with fresh arugula or watercress.
4 Top carefully with the muffin lids to serve.

Cherry Tomato and Basil Clafoutis

Traditional French clafouti *is a lightly cooked batter dessert studded with cherries—like a soft, custardy pancake. This savory version, using tomatoes, Parmesan cheese, and basil, makes a satisfying first course.*

PREPARATION: 10 MINUTES
BAKING: 20 MINUTES
SERVES 6

Butter for greasing
$1^1/_2$ pounds cherry tomatoes
4 eggs
2 tablespoons all-purpose flour
$^3/_4$ cup crème fraîche or sour cream
4 tablespoons milk
Good handful fresh basil, roughly torn
$^1/_2$ cup grated Parmesan cheese
Salt and pepper

1 Preheat the oven to 375°F. Lightly grease 6 gratin dishes, 5 inches long and 1 inch deep, with butter, and spread the tomatoes over the bottoms. Beat the eggs in a large bowl, then beat in the flour using a wire whisk. Beat in the crème fraîche or sour cream and the milk until the batter is smooth. Stir in the basil and all but 1 tablespoon of the Parmesan; season.
2 Pour the batter over the tomatoes and sprinkle with the remaining cheese and an extra grinding of pepper. Bake for 20 minutes until puffed up and golden on top.
3 Serve warm with a green salad.

VARIATION: To make one large clafouti to serve 3 to 4 people as a lunch dish, put 1 pound small tomatoes in a 9-inch quiche dish. Follow the recipe above, but bake for 30 to 35 minutes.

Tarragon Mushrooms with Bean Mashed Potatoes

PREPARATION: 15 MINUTES
COOKING: 20 MINUTES
SERVES 4

1 tablespoon olive oil
1 large Spanish onion, sliced
2 tablespoons cornstarch
$2^1/_2$ cups vegetable stock
6 tablespoons dry sherry
8 mushrooms
Sprig fresh tarragon, stalks removed
3 large potatoes, peeled and diced
1 garlic clove, thinly sliced
1 (14 ounce) can flageolet or cannellini beans, drained and rinsed
3 scallions, minced
3 tablespoons milk
Salt and pepper

1 Heat the olive oil in a skillet. Add the onion and sauté for 2 to 3 minutes until soft.
2 Mix the cornstarch with a little of the vegetable stock to make a thin, smooth paste. Stir into the remaining stock with the sherry. Pour over the onion and bring to a boil. Lower the heat and simmer, stirring constantly, for 2 to 3 minutes, until thick.
3 Push the mushrooms under the surface of the sauce. Sprinkle the tarragon over and simmer for 10 minutes.
4 Meanwhile, cook the diced potatoes and garlic in lightly salted boiling water for 8 minutes. Add the beans and cook for 2 minutes longer; drain and mash. Stir in the scallions and milk; beat until smooth. Season to taste.
5 Serve immediately, with the tarragon-flavored mushrooms and sauce spooned over.

Warm Poached Eggs on Potato Salad

PREPARATION: 25 MINUTES
COOKING: ABOUT 20 MINUTES
SERVES 4

$^2/_3$ cup white wine vinegar

4 eggs

Handful each arugula and baby spinach leaves

1 tablespoon olive oil

FOR THE POTATO SALAD:

1 pound new potatoes

1 tablespoon olive oil

Juice of 1 lime

1 tablespoon minced shallot

2 to 3 tablespoons crème fraîche or sour cream

FOR THE GREEN BUTTER:

$^1/_2$ cup finely shredded sorrel leaves or 1 tablespoon chopped tarragon

4 tablespoons butter, softened

Squeeze fresh lemon juice (a little more if you're using tarragon)

Coarse sea salt and pepper

1 Bring a large pan of water to a simmer and add the vinegar. One at a time, break the eggs into a cup and slowly slip them into the pan; cook for 3 minutes. Using a slotted spoon, transfer immediately to a bowl of ice water.
2 To make the potato salad, first boil the potatoes for about 15 minutes until tender. Then drain, peel, and mash roughly with a fork. Stir in remaining ingredients and season; mix well.
3 To make the green butter, mash the herbs with the butter, lemon juice, and salt and pepper; set aside (do not chill).
4 Sit a 3-inch ring mold on each plate and spoon in the potato, pressing down well (or spoon a neat mound on the plate). Toss the arugula and spinach in the olive oil and season. Lay across the potato or scatter around the edge.
5 Bring a pan of water to a simmer. Remove the eggs from the ice water and carefully neaten with scissors. Plunge into the simmering water for 1 minute to reheat. Sit them on the potato salad and spoon the butter over. Serve sprinkled with salt.

Grilled Sweet Potato and Beet Salad

You can also cook the sweet potato on the grill until deliciously charred and tender—perfect for warm days when you want to dine alfresco.

PREPARATION: 20 MINUTES
BROILING: 20 MINUTES
SERVES 4

2 pounds sweet potatoes, unpeeled

Salt and pepper

2 tablespoons olive oil

$1^1/_2$ pounds fresh cooked baby beets, halved

$1^3/_4$ ounces arugula leaves

1 tablespoon pine nuts, toasted

FOR THE DRESSING:

2 teaspoons prepared horseradish

4 tablespoons sour cream

2 tablespoons chopped fresh dill

1 Preheat the broiler. Cut the sweet potatoes into slices about $^1/_2$ inch thick, then cut each slice in half again. Lightly sprinkle each slice with salt and pepper. Brush with the oil and place in the broiler pan. Broil the potatoes for 10 minutes on each side until tender. For the final 5 minutes of broiling, add the beets to the broiler pan and toss in the oil. (To prevent the color of the beets from bleeding into the potato, move the potato slices to one end of the pan.)
2 Arrange the arugula leaves either in a large serving dish or on individual plates. Mix the dressing ingredients together until thoroughly combined and season to taste. Top the arugula leaves with the potato slices and beet halves. Drizzle the dressing over the top and scatter the pine nuts over. Serve immediately.

Piedmontese Peppers

For this recipe, a hot oven is absolutely essential to roast the peppers and tomatoes to a tender texture and for the sweet flavor to develop. Serve the peppers hot or cold, scattered with the fresh herbs, or add a few teaspoons of capers and chopped pitted ripe olives.

PREPARATION: 10 MINUTES

BAKING: 15 TO 20 MINUTES

SERVES 2

2 red bell peppers

2 garlic cloves, sliced

2 plum tomatoes, halved

2 tablespoons extra-virgin olive oil

Salt and pepper

Handful fresh basil leaves, roughly chopped

1 tablespoon roughly chopped fresh oregano

1 Preheat the oven to 425°F. Halve the peppers and remove the seeds but not the stems. Place the peppers skin-side down on a lightly greased cookie sheet. Place slices of garlic inside each pepper half and top each with a tomato half, cut-side down. Drizzle with the oil and season. Bake for about 10 minutes.

2 Reduce the oven setting to 400°F and continue baking for 15 to 20 minutes longer, until the peppers and tomatoes are tender.

3 Serve hot or cold, scattered with the fresh herbs.

Warm Maple-Glazed Vegetable Salad with Feta and Walnuts

This simple hot salad makes an interesting light supper, served with warm walnut bread. You can assemble the paper packages in advance.

PREPARATION: 15 MINUTES

COOKING: 30 MINUTES

SERVES 4

12 ounces small new potatoes

5 ounces pearl onions or shallots

1 cup cubed feta cheese

1 cup frozen fava beans

4 ounces baby corn, halved lengthwise

4 ounces sugar snap peas

$1/2$ cup walnuts, lightly toasted

Grated zest of 1 orange

3 tablespoons roughly chopped fresh parsley

1-inch piece ginger root, peeled and grated

Salt and pepper

5 tablespoons maple syrup

2 teaspoons olive oil

1 Steam the potatoes and onions or shallots in a steamer over boiling water for about 20 minutes until just tender; reserve the water for later use.

2 Cut out four 13-inch circles from waxed or parchment paper. In a bowl, toss the potatoes and onions with the feta, fava beans, corn, sugar snap peas, walnuts, orange zest, parsley, ginger, and seasoning. Divide among the paper circles.

3 Mix together the maple syrup and oil and spoon over the vegetables and other ingredients. Bring the paper up over the filling and twist together to seal.

4 Place the paper packages in the steamer rack and cover tightly. Steam for 10 minutes. To test that the vegetables are just tender, unwrap one package and pierce the vegetables. If necessary, re-wrap and steam for a little longer.

5 Serve the vegetables in the packages.

Freshness is paramount when buying beans; any showing signs of limpness or shriveling are definite rejects. Look for smooth, firm specimens that snap cleanly when bent. Green beans should not be discolored or coarse. Chinese yard-long beans should be a bright grassy green. Don't worry about brown flecks on yard-longs—these are part of the pigmentation and will disappear during cooking. Beans in prime condition will keep for 3 to 4 days in a plastic bag in the refrigerator.

If your beans need stringing, snap off both ends, pulling them back along the length of the bean to remove the strings. Or, in the case of flat runner beans, use a swivel-blade vegetable peeler. If the beans are stringless, line them up a handful at a time and chop off the stem ends. You can remove the slender growing tips of French-style green beans if you wish. Leave the beans whole if they seem tender enough; otherwise cut them into short pieces.

Beans

Salted Beans

Salting green or runner beans is an excellent preservative and an alternative to freezing—the result is crisp, fresh beans throughout the fall and winter.

1 Wash and trim 3 pounds beans and cut into 1-inch diagonal slices.
2 Sprinkle a $^1/_2$-inch layer of coarse sea salt into a wide-necked 1 quart canning jar. Cover with a 1 inch layer of beans; repeat each step until the jar is full.
3 Push the beans down to pack tightly and cover the jar with waxed paper. Loosely secure with string and leave for 2 days.
4 After 2 days, the beans will have settled. Add more layers, cover with waxed paper, and seal with a nonmetallic lid. Keep in a cool, dark place for up to 6 months.
5 To use, remove the amount of beans you need and rinse in a colander under cold water. Soak in plenty of fresh water for 2 hours. Drain, rinse, and boil for 4 to 5 minutes until tender.

Vegetable Salad with Curry-Soy Vinaigrette

This delightful warm vegetable salad has a bold dressing. The idea is French, but the enticing flavors are exotically Asian. Look in Chinese food stores for fresh water chestnuts.

PREPARATION: 10 MINUTES
COOKING: 10 MINUTES
SERVES 4

$1/2$ pound ripe tomatoes

4 ounces broccoli, cut into small florets

4 ounces green beans, trimmed

4 ounces cauliflower, cut into small florets

1 cup shelled fresh or frozen peas

$1/3$ cup peeled and sliced fresh water chestnuts

3 tablespoons minced shallots, squeezed dry

3 tablespoons finely snipped chives

FOR THE CURRY-SOY VINAIGRETTE:

2 teaspoons Dijon mustard

2 teaspoons Madras or mild curry powder

2 tablespoons soy sauce

2 teaspoons salt, or to taste

1 teaspoon freshly ground Chinese five-spice powder or black pepper

4 tablespoons extra-virgin olive oil

1 To make the vinaigrette, beat all the ingredients together in a bowl; set aside.
2 Drop the tomatoes into a pan of boiling, salted water for 5 seconds; remove them with a slotted spoon. Skin the tomatoes and remove the seeds. Cut the flesh into $1^{1}/_{2}$-inch pieces; set aside.
3 Add the broccoli, beans, and cauliflower to the pan, and cook for 3 minutes. Add the peas and cook for 1 minute longer. Drain the vegetables and put them in a warm bowl. Add the tomatoes and water chestnuts.
4 Drizzle in the vinaigrette and add the shallots and chives. Mix well to serve.

Three-Bean Salad with Citrus Dressing

This colorful appetizer or side dish is easily turned into a main course by adding 1 (14 ounce) can well-drained tuna chunks, or $1^{1}/_{2}$ cups feta cheese cubes. Its fabulous flavor is enhanced by dark sesame oil—or use hazelnut or walnut oil.

PREPARATION: 20 MINUTES
COOKING: 8 MINUTES
SERVES 4

$1/2$ pound green or runner beans

$1/2$ pound French-style green beans, halved

3 cups shelled fava beans or fresh peas

Bunch scallions, sliced

8 radishes, halved

1 tablespoon snipped fresh chives

Juice and finely grated zest of 1 small orange

3 tablespoons olive oil

1 tablespoon sesame oil

Salt and pepper

$2/3$ cup plain yogurt

2 tablespoons chopped fresh mint

1 Trim the green or runner beans and remove the strings; cut into 1-inch slices. Cook in boiling, salted water for 4 minutes. Add the French-style beans and fava beans or peas, and cook for 4 minutes, or until just tender; drain and refresh in cold water.
2 Put the beans in a large bowl. Add the scallions, radishes, and chives. Mix together the orange juice, oils, and salt and pepper. Pour this over the vegetables and toss.
3 Mix together the orange zest, yogurt, and mint. Divide the bean salad among plates and spoon the citrus dressing on top.

Salad Dressings

What do you put on a salad before tossing it? A vinaigrette dressing, oil-and-vinegar dressing, or Italian dressing? Just a few terms for what are basically the same thing. And once you've perfected a basic dressing, you can head off in all sorts of flavor directions.

Just scan any supermarket aisle of bottled dressings and you'll see the potential—from sun-dried tomato, Caesar-style, and Italian, to zesty garlic, lime and dill, honey and mustard, sesame and ginger, and toasted onion.

You can easily make all these and more, for a fraction of the price and with a better flavor.

MIXING THE DRESSING

The neatest and easiest way is to measure your ingredients into a jar, close with a lid, and shake vigorously like a cocktail; this makes the oil and vinegar emulsify into a glossy thick liquid. The jar should have a wide neck or you'll have to use a funnel, and it should be roomy so the contents get thoroughly mixed.

It also needs to fit comfortably in your hand (so you can shake it easily) and should have a secure lid, preferably with a screw-top. After shaking, the dressing gradually separates, but it will emulsify again in a couple of shakes.

Dressings are best made fresh, but you can chill any left over for up to 3 days—bring to room temperature before using because the oil thickens, even solidifies, in the refrigerator.

Not all dressings have to be mixed before use. If you sprinkle the oil and vinegar separately over the plate, you can create a pretty pattern. Use differently flavored and colored oils and vinegars, such as raspberry vinegar with walnut oil. A few drops of balsamic vinegar contrasts well with a flavored olive oil.

For mixed greens, dressings should be tossed in just before serving so the leaves retain their crispness. Italian cooks don't always bother to mix the dressing at all—they just squeeze lemon juice over the leaves, drizzle over the oil, and toss together. Another idea is to pour the dressing into the salad bowl—or even mix it in the bowl—drop the leaves on top and toss.

TRANSFORMING DRESSINGS

Before taking your basic dressing a step further, consider what it is going to be poured over or tossed with. The flavors should blend harmoniously and not clash or overpower each other.

Green leaves benefit from a sprinkling of chopped herbs, such as chives, parsley, or tarragon. Be braver with stronger-flavored vegetables, meat, or fish—add creamed horseradish, crushed garlic, finely chopped capers or anchovies, or a robust mustard.

Change the flavor and texture of a dressing completely with piquant blue cheeses such as Stilton, Roquefort, or Danish blue; and serve with a mixture of salad greens and toasted nuts, such as hazelnuts or walnuts, and chicken. (Use a lighter oil than olive with cheese.)

Then there are creamy dressings made with half dressing and half mayonnaise, sour cream, or yogurt. Their smoothness makes them ideal for spooning over warm new potatoes and beans, cold poached chicken, or salmon. Vary creamy dressings and add color and texture by blending them in a food processor with fresh herbs, watercress, roasted bell peppers, or skinned and seeded tomatoes.

Dressings can be served warm. Either add warm cooking juices to the vinaigrette, as in a chicken liver salad or seafood salad, or heat the dressing in the pan you used for cooking (for instance, if you've been frying shrimp, chicken, or bacon). A particularly delicious classic warm dressing is Sauce Vierge (right).

MAKING A PERFECT DRESSING

There are no set rules about which oils and vinegars to use. A basic dressing is three parts oil to one part vinegar or lemon juice (this is just a guide–some people tone down the vinegar by adding more oil), and salt and pepper to taste.

WHICH OIL?

Olive oil is the traditional choice, but you can lighten its taste by mixing it with a milder-flavored one, such as sunflower. If you decide to use a stronger-flavored oil, such as walnut or hazelnut, you may want to tone it down by mixing with a blander oil, such as peanut.

WHICH VINEGAR?

Red or white wine and the sweet balsamic are the most popular, but try another flavored variety. Tarragon vinegar, for example, goes well with a chicken salad, while fruit vinegars, such as raspberry and black currant, are beautiful in a warm dressing for roast meats, particularly game.

ANYTHING ELSE?

You can add a teaspoon of mustard or cream to help the oil and vinegar combine, but it's not essential. Some chefs add a few drops of water to delay the vinegar hitting the palate before the softer oil; it certainly makes a sharp dressing taste milder.

SAUCE VIERGE

Heat 4 tablespoons olive oil, 1 tablespoon wine vinegar, and 8 lightly crushed coriander seeds to infuse. Toss in 4 finely chopped tomatoes (skinned and seeded) and 1 tablespoon each chopped chervil, parsley, and tarragon. Cook very briefly and spoon over broiled shrimp or scallops or lightly steamed vegetables.

Dandelion Leaves with Pear, Roquefort, and Hazelnuts

The creaminess of the blue cheese contrasts well with the bitterness of the leaves and the crunch of the hazelnuts.

PREPARATION: 15 MINUTES

SERVES 4

1 ripe pear

1 teaspoon fresh lemon juice

1 head radicchio, coarsely chopped

1 head Belgian endive, leaves torn

Handful (about 1$\frac{1}{2}$ ounces) dandelion
    leaves or watercress

4 ounces Roquefort or other blue cheese

2 tablespoons hazelnut oil

2 tablespoons extra-virgin olive oil

4 teaspoons balsamic vinegar

Salt and pepper

$\frac{1}{2}$ cup roughly chopped toasted hazelnuts

1 Peel, halve, and core the pear. Cut the flesh into $\frac{1}{4}$-inch dice. Toss with the lemon juice to stop the pear from discoloring; set aside.

2 Put the radicchio, endive, and dandelion leaves or watercress in a large serving bowl. Add the pear and crumble the cheese over.

3 Whisk the two oils with the balsamic vinegar and season with salt and pepper. Pour over the salad.

4 Sprinkle with the nuts and toss everything together to serve.

French Lentil Salad

The lentils will absorb the flavors of the dressing. You can use other lentils than the small green ones from Puy, in France, but be careful not to overcook them.

PREPARATION: 15 MINUTES

COOKING: 30 MINUTES

SERVES 8

1¼ cups French lentils, rinsed

1 red onion, cut into thin wedges

1 red bell pepper, seeded and diced

Bunch flat-leaf parsley, chopped

FOR THE DRESSING:

7 tablespoons virgin olive oil

3 tablespoons cider vinegar

2 teaspoons tamari sauce

2 teaspoons Dijon mustard

2 small garlic cloves, crushed

Salt and pepper

1 To make the dressing, mix together all the ingredients; set aside.

2 Place the lentils in a pan. Cover with water and bring to a boil. Boil rapidly for 5 minutes, lower the heat, and simmer for 20 minutes, until just tender.

3 Drain the lentils thoroughly and return to the pan. Stir in the dressing. Leave to cool, stirring occasionally, so the lentils absorb the dressing.

4 When cold, stir in the red onion, bell pepper, and parsley. Season to taste and serve.

Tamari and Toasted Seed Coleslaw

Tamari sauce is wheat-free and very dark in color. It is thicker and has a stronger flavor than soy sauce. You can also use this mixture of toasted mixed seeds and tamari sauce as a coating for veggie burgers.

PREPARATION: 15 MINUTES

COOKING: 3 MINUTES

SERVES 4

2 cups mixed seeds, such as sunflower or sesame

2 tablespoons tamari sauce

5½ cups shredded green cabbage

3 carrots, grated

3 scallions, minced

⅔ cup mayonnaise

1 teaspoon whole-grain mustard

3 tablespoons sunflower oil

1 tablespoon white wine vinegar

Salt and pepper

1 In a dry skillet, toast the mixed seeds for 2 to 3 minutes, stirring frequently, until light brown. Sprinkle the tamari over and toss together quickly; the seeds will stick together initially, but as the mixture dries the seeds will separate.

2 Combine all the vegetables in a large bowl. Mix together the mayonnaise, mustard, oil, vinegar, and freshly ground black pepper. Stir into the vegetables with the cooled seed mixture and toss well. Season to taste, remembering that tamari sauce is salty.

Asparagus, Sea Kale, and Red Onion Salad with Spicy Potato Croutons and Sour Cream and Chive Dressing

PREPARATION: ABOUT 30 MINUTES

COOKING: ABOUT 20 MINUTES

SERVES 4

12 to 16 asparagus stalks

Salt and pepper

Bunch sea kale or 4 celery stalks

4 tablespoons olive or peanut oil

$1/4$ teaspoon curry powder

1 baked potato, peeled and cut into
   $1/4$-inch cubes

Juice of 1 lime

4 to 5 tablespoons sour cream

1 heaped teaspoon finely snipped fresh chives

2 small red onions, thinly sliced and
   separated into rings

Handful salad greens, such as arugula,
   spinach, and watercress

12 small sorrel leaves

16 to 20 cilantro leaves

1 Lightly peel the asparagus and trim off the woody ends. Plunge the stalks into a deep pan of boiling, salted water for 2 to 3 minutes until tender. (Lift one from the water with a spoon and pinch lightly—if it is cooked, the asparagus will just start to give.) It's best to leave them with a slight bite for a better texture and flavor. Once cooked, refresh in ice water. Cut each stalk diagonally in half. Remove the base of the sea kale's stalk, then leave whole or cut diagonally in half. If using celery, cut the stalks into sticks.

2 Heat 2 tablespoons of the oil in a skillet. Sprinkle the curry powder over the potato cubes, making sure they are all evenly seasoned. Fry the potatoes slowly until golden and crisp. Once cooked, drain and season with a pinch of salt; reserve the oil for the dressing.

3 In a bowl, mix the remaining oil with the curried oil and a little lime juice. Place the sour cream in a separate bowl, season with salt and pepper, and loosen the consistency with a little lime juice. Stir in the snipped chives.

4 Put the asparagus, sea kale, onion rings, and salad greens in a bowl. Drizzle a few drops of the curried oil dressing over and toss. Divide the dressed salad among serving plates and spoon some sour cream and chive dressing around the edge. Scatter the sorrel and cilantro leaves and hot, crisp, potato croutons over the salad. Serve immediately.

Butter Bean, Olive, and Feta Salad

PREPARATION: ABOUT 15 MINUTES

SERVES 4

4 tomatoes

4 tablespoons olive oil

Juice of 1 lemon

2 (14 ounce) cans butter or lima beans, drained

$1/3$ cup pitted ripe olives

1 small red onion, thinly sliced

$1^1/2$ cups crumbled feta cheese

Handful chopped fresh parsley

Salt and pepper

1 Chop one of the tomatoes. Put it in a food processor or blender with the olive oil and lemon juice, and process until fairly smooth.

2 Cut the remaining tomatoes into wedges. Mix the tomato wedges with the beans, olives, onion, feta, parsley, and salt and pepper to taste.

3 Toss in the tomato dressing. Serve with pita bread.

Caesar Salad with Parmesan Chips

Some people don't like the raw egg in the original Caesar salad. This version removes that element from the dressing—and it still tastes great. Instead of Parmesan, cheddar can be used for the chips.

PREPARATION: 15 MINUTES

BAKING: 15 TO 20 MINUTES

SERVES 4

1 head Romaine lettuce, torn into bite-size pieces and chilled

5 canned anchovy fillets, drained and minced

1 garlic clove, minced

3 tablespoons olive oil

8 slices French bread

2 sheets rice paper

$^1/_2$ cup freshly grated Parmesan cheese

FOR THE DRESSING:

2 teaspoons Dijon mustard

1 teaspoon sugar

1 tablespoon white wine vinegar

5 tablespoons olive oil

2 tablespoons crème fraîche or sour cream

Salt and pepper

Dash Worcestershire sauce

1 Preheat the oven to 350°F.

2 In a bowl, mix the anchovies, garlic, and oil to a paste. Spread this over each slice of bread. Bake for 15 to 20 minutes until crisp. Cut the toasts into large bite-size pieces.

3 Meanwhile, line a small cookie sheet with the rice paper sheets and sprinkle them with Parmesan. Bake above the toasts for 15 to 20 minutes until the cheese melts, and is crisp and pale golden. Leave to cool, then break into pieces.

4 To make the dressing, first whisk together the mustard, sugar, and vinegar, then gradually whisk in the oil. Whisk in the crème fraîche or sour cream, season, and add a dash of Worcestershire sauce.

5 Mix together the lettuce, toasts, and Parmesan chips. Drizzle the dressing over them. Toss well and serve on 4 plates.

Mediterranean Salad

PREPARATION: 30 MINUTES

BAKING: 30 TO 40 MINUTES

SERVES 4

2 yellow bell peppers, halved and seeded

1 red bell pepper, halved and seeded

3 garlic cloves, unpeeled

1 red onion, thinly sliced

$^1/_2$ cucumber, peeled and diced

6 plum tomatoes, cut into wedges

12 pitted ripe olives

Handful fresh basil, roughly torn

2 tablespoons chopped fresh dill or parsley

1 tablespoon chopped fresh oregano

Salt and pepper

FOR THE CROUTONS:

$^1/_2$ pound firm country bread, thickly sliced and crusts removed

2 tablespoons butter, melted

FOR THE DRESSING:

5 tablespoons extra-virgin olive oil

1 to 2 tablespoons balsamic vinegar

1 teaspoon Dijon mustard

Salt and pepper

1 Preheat the oven to 400°F and preheat the broiler to high. Place the peppers, skin side up, on the broiler rack with the garlic cloves, and broil for 10 to 15 minutes, turning the garlic occasionally, until the peppers are blistered and black all over. Remove the garlic if it starts burning. When cool, peel the peppers and cut the flesh into thin strips. Place in a salad bowl. Set the garlic aside.

2 Add the onion, cucumber, tomatoes, olives, and herbs to the salad bowl. Season and toss lightly to mix.

3 To make the croutons, first brush the bread on both sides with butter, cut into cubes, and arrange in one layer on a cookie sheet. Toast for 10 to 12 minutes until golden— check frequently after 8 minutes because they color quickly.

4 To make the dressing, peel the garlic and mash in a bowl; gradually whisk in the oil, vinegar, mustard, and seasoning.

5 Drizzle the dressing over the salad and toss well. Sprinkle the bread cubes over.

The oven can help bring out the best in vegetables—and not simply as roasted vegetables: Bake them slowly in rich sauces to bring out their full flavors; encase them in crisp pastry for a delicious texture contrast; or stuff them with a range of fillings to produce hearty, warming family fare.

Putting on the Heat

Bakes, Gratins, Pies, and Tarts

Macaroni and Cheese Pies with Artichokes and Mushrooms

Here is the most luscious version of macaroni and cheese ever devised. All the elements can be prepared ahead and assembled just before serving. What makes this dish so special is the inclusion of three sauces—Mornay (a cheesy white sauce), a Parmesan sauce made with cream, and a hollandaise sauce. Here you can make a shortcut by replacing the hollandaise with two egg yolks. The recipe uses canned artichokes, but you can always use cooked fresh globe artichokes if you prefer.

PREPARATION: 20 MINUTES

COOKING: ABOUT 55 MINUTES

SERVES 4

2 tablespoons butter, plus more for greasing

1 pound puff or pie pastry dough, defrosted if frozen

1 cup macaroni, cooked, drained, and cooled

$1/2$ pound canned artichokes, drained, or 2 cooked globe artichokes

4 ounces crimini or button mushrooms, quartered

$2/3$ cup Hollandaise Sauce (page 44) or 2 egg yolks

2 heaped tablespoons softly whipped cream

FOR THE MORNAY SAUCE:

1 tablespoon butter

2 tablespoons all-purpose flour

$3/4$ cup plus 2 tablespoons milk

Salt and pepper

$1/2$ teaspoon prepared English mustard

$3/4$ cup grated cheddar cheese

FOR THE PARMESAN SAUCE:

$1 1/4$ cups heavy cream

$3/4$ cup freshly grated Parmesan cheese

2 tablespoons crème fraîche or sour cream

Lemon juice, to taste

TO SERVE:

Tossed green salad, flavored with balsamic vinaigrette, sliced red onions, watercress, and walnuts

1 Preheat the oven to 400°F. Lightly butter four 4-inch round pastry rings ($2 1/2$ inches deep) and sit them on a cookie sheet lined with waxed paper. Roll out the dough to a thickness of about $1/16$ inch and cut out four 4-inch circles. Sit one in each ring. Roll out the remaining dough and cut into strips wide enough to line the sides of the rings. Once in place, press the dough along the bottom edge to seal with the base, then all the way around the sides so it comes a little above the ring.

2 Line each mold with foil and fill with baking beans or rice. Leave to rest in the refrigerator for 20 minutes, then bake blind for 15 to 20 minutes until a light golden color; this will guarantee a crisp finish. Remove from the oven and take out the foil and beans; set aside until ready to use.

3 To make the Mornay sauce, first melt the butter in a small pan, then add the flour and cook over low heat for a few minutes without letting it color. Meanwhile, warm the milk in a separate pan. Gradually ladle the milk into the flour, stirring constantly to make a smooth sauce. Simmer for 20 to 25 minutes until thick and smooth. Season with salt and pepper to taste. Stir in the mustard and grated cheese and heat slowly, stirring, until the cheese melts. Pass the sauce through a strainer into a bowl and cover until needed. Reheat very slowly, without boiling.

4 To make the Parmesan sauce, first pour the cream into a large pan and bring to a boil. Then lower the heat and whisk in the Parmesan and crème fraîche or sour cream. Add the lemon juice and salt and pepper to taste. Stir in the cool, cooked macaroni and warm through.

5 To assemble the pies, first warm the pastry cases in the oven and preheat the broiler. Then melt the 2 tablespoons butter in a skillet. Cut the artichokes into 8 to 12 wedges and cook in the butter with the mushrooms for 5 minutes until golden brown. Stir into the macaroni mixture and adjust the seasoning. Divide among the pastry cases.

6 Stir the hollandaise sauce or egg yolks and the whipped cream into the Mornay sauce and spoon into the pies. Broil for 3 to 4 minutes until dark golden. Serve the pies immediately. Serve with a tossed salad flavored with balsamic vinaigrette, sliced red onions, watercress, and walnuts.

Leek and Potato Pie

PREPARATION: ABOUT 35 MINUTES

BAKING: 30 TO 40 MINUTES

SERVES 8

6 tablespoons butter

5 cups trimmed and sliced leeks

2 cups dry hard cider

2 cups heavy cream

2 teaspoons whole-grain mustard

2 eggs, beaten

1¼ cups grated cheddar cheese

1 pound potatoes, cut into ¼-inch-thick slices
   (no need to peel)

Salt and pepper

12 sheets of phyllo pastry dough, each about
   14 × 10 inches, defrosted if frozen

1 Preheat the oven to 350°F. Melt one-third of the butter in a large skillet. Add the leeks and sauté for 6 to 8 minutes until soft, stirring occasionally. Add the cider, bring to a boil, and boil rapidly, uncovered, until reduced by about two-thirds. Add the cream, return to a boil, and boil rapidly for 3 to 5 minutes, until the sauce reaches the consistency of thick cream. Remove from the heat and stir in the mustard, eggs, and cheese.

2 Meanwhile, cook the potatoes in boiling salted water for 3 to 4 minutes until tender; be sure they are cooked through, because the acidity from the cider will prevent them from cooking further when added to the sauce. Drain and stir gently with the leek mixture. Season to taste.

3 Melt the remaining butter. Use a little to brush the bottom of a 13 × 9-inch baking dish. Place a sheet of phyllo pastry dough on top and brush with a little more butter. Repeat with 4 more sheets of dough to cover the bottom and sides of the dish, overlapping the edges. Spread the filling inside, then layer another 5 sheets of dough, in the same way, over the top; fold over any overlapping dough. Brush 2 more sheets with the remaining butter, gently crumple, and place on top of the pie.

4 Bake for 30 to 40 minutes until golden.

Summer Vegetable Lattice Tart

PREPARATION: 50 TO 55 MINUTES
PLUS RISING

BAKING: 20 TO 25 MINUTES

SERVES 6

Vegetable oil for greasing

1²/₃ cups bread flour

¹/₄-ounce envelope quick-rising active dry yeast

1 teaspoon light brown sugar

Salt and pepper

²/₃ cup warm water (115°F)

1 egg, beaten, for glazing

Coarse sea salt for sprinkling

¹/₂ ounce fresh basil, stems removed, to serve

FOR THE FILLING:

3 cups sliced onions

3 garlic cloves, crushed

1¹/₄ cups vegetable stock

¹/₂ ounce fresh rosemary sprigs, stems removed

1 orange, 1 red, and 1 yellow bell pepper,
    seeded and cut into chunks

6 plum tomatoes, quartered and seeded

4 ounces asparagus tips

Salt and pepper

1 Lightly grease a 13 × 9-inch baking dish. Sift the flour into a large bowl and stir in the yeast, sugar, and a good pinch each of salt and freshly ground black pepper. Gradually stir in the water to form a soft dough. Turn out onto a lightly floured surface and knead for 10 minutes until smooth and elastic. Return to the bowl, cover with plastic wrap, and leave to rise in a warm place for about 1 hour or until doubled in size.

2 Meanwhile, make the filling: Place the onions, garlic, stock, and half the rosemary in a large pan. Bring to a boil. Lower the heat and simmer for 15 to 20 minutes, stirring occasionally, until all the stock has been absorbed; set aside.

3 Preheat the oven to 425°F. Turn the dough out onto a lightly floured surface; cut off one-third and reserve. Roll out the remaining dough into a 14 × 10-inch rectangle and use to line the baking pan.

4 Spoon the onion mixture over the dough. Scatter the peppers, tomatoes, asparagus, and black pepper over. Cut the reserved dough into 8 pieces and roll each to make a long "rope." Arrange in a lattice pattern over the filling and pinch the ends into the tart to seal. Brush with the egg and sprinkle the salt over.

5 Bake for 20 to 25 minutes until golden. Scatter the basil over; serve the tart either hot or cold.

Roasted Vegetable Quiche

PREPARATION: 20 MINUTES

BAKING: 1 HOUR

SERVES 6

2 zucchini, sliced

1 red and 1 yellow bell pepper, seeded

1 tablespoon olive oil

All-purpose flour for dusting

Pastry for single pie crust

1 large egg

1 cup crème fraîche or sour cream

12 fresh basil leaves

Salt and pepper

1 Preheat the oven to 400°F. Toss the zucchini and thickly sliced peppers in the oil in a roasting pan. Roast for 20 minutes, stirring halfway through. Remove from the oven and set aside to cool slightly.

2 Put a 9-inch tart ring on a cookie sheet. On a lightly floured surface, roll out the dough into a 12-inch circle. Place the dough in the tart ring so the sides of the ring support the dough. Spoon the vegetables into the middle of the dough circle and spread out to within 2 inches of the edge.

3 Beat together the egg and crème fraîche or sour cream. Tear in the basil and season. Pour over the roast vegetables, fold the dough edges over, and pinch the tucks in the dough together. Bake for 40 to 45 minutes, until the filling is set.

4 Serve warm or at room temperature.

Provençale Tartlets with Pesto Sauce

If you want to make your own puff pastry, go ahead; otherwise buy a good-quality frozen dough. This recipe is for 4 tartlets, but you can make one 8-inch tart—in which case it will take about 45 minutes to bake. The vegetables and pastry cases can be baked up to 2 days in advance and kept in the refrigerator. If you do this, warm the vegetables through before you add the egg and cream mixture. The sauce is an optional extra; if you prefer, serve the tart with a crisp salad.

PREPARATION: 40 MINUTES

BAKING: 35 MINUTES

SERVES 4

1/2 pound puff pastry dough, defrosted if frozen

1 tablespoon unsalted butter

3 tablespoons olive oil, plus more for drizzling

2 large onions, sliced

2 red bell peppers and 2 green bell peppers, seeded and sliced

1 garlic clove, crushed

1 egg

2/3 cup heavy cream

1 tablespoon freshly grated Parmesan cheese

Salt and pepper

2 zucchini, thinly sliced diagonally

4 ripe plum tomatoes, sliced

FOR THE SAUCE:

1 tablespoon pesto

2/3 cup mayonnaise

1 Preheat the oven to 400°F. Roll out the dough on a lightly floured surface and use to line four 4-inch individual tartlet pans. Line the dough with foil, fill with baking beans, and bake for about 15 minutes. Remove from the oven and remove the paper and beans.

2 Meanwhile, melt the butter with 2 tablespoons of the oil. Add the sliced onions, peppers, and crushed garlic and sauté for 6 to 8 minutes until soft. Leave to cool for a few minutes.

3 Whisk the egg with the cream, Parmesan, and salt and pepper to taste. Stir into the onion mixture. Cook over low heat, stirring, until thick, for 10 to 15 minutes; leave to cool.

4 Heat 1 tablespoon of oil in a pan. Add the zucchini slices and cook until they are light brown, 3 to 4 minutes. Divide the onion, pepper, and garlic mixture among the tartlets. Arrange alternating rows of tomato and zucchini slices on top.

5 Reduce the oven temperature to 350°F and bake the tartlets for about 20 minutes.

6 Make the sauce: Mix the pesto into the mayonnaise. Spoon the mixture onto 4 serving plates. Remove the tartlets from the pans and drizzle a little olive oil over the top of each one. Set the tarts on top of the pools of pesto sauce and serve.

VARIATIONS: For striking color combinations, try yellow summer squash or 1 each of summer squash and zucchini, either alternating slices of different color or making 2 differently colored types of tartlet. You can use sun-dried tomato paste or black olive paste if you are not a pesto fan.

Goat Cheese and Onion Tartlets

These make an attractive first course, whether the party is for 6 or 26. The tarts can be assembled ahead of time and frozen, and baked when needed. To prepare ahead, make up to the end of Step 3, cover, and chill for up to 4 hours ahead; or prepare up to the end of Step 3, freeze on cookie sheets, then wrap in foil and freeze for up to 3 months. To bake, first defrost on cookie sheets for 2 hours. You need a firm goat cheese that slices easily.

PREPARATION: 35 MINUTES

BAKING: 20 MINUTES

SERVES 6

2 red onions, thinly sliced

2 tablespoons olive oil

1 tablespoon balsamic vinegar

Salt and pepper

$^1/_2$ pound puff pastry dough, defrosted if frozen

2 firm goat cheeses, each 4 ounces in weight,
    at room temperature

4 ounces chicory or frisée

2 teaspoons fresh lemon juice

3 tablespoons olive oil

$^1/_2$ cup chopped walnuts

1 Preheat the oven to 425°F. Sauté the onions slowly in the oil for 10 minutes. Add the vinegar and salt and pepper, and cook for 5 minutes until just caramelized.

2 Roll out the dough and trim to 8 × 12 inches. Cut out six 4-inch squares. Put on a damp cookie sheet; score lightly $^1/_2$ inch inside each square; do not cut through.

3 Spread the onions within this area. Use a serrated knife to cut off the ends of the cheeses; slice each into 3 pieces. Put a slice on each tartlet.

4 Bake for 20 minutes until the pastry puffs up.

5 Toss the chicory with the lemon juice, olive oil, and salt and pepper. Sprinkle the walnuts over to serve with the tartlets.

French Onion Tart

No fussing with tart pans here—this tart is baked on a cookie sheet with the filling piled on top.

PREPARATION: 30 MINUTES

BAKING: 20 TO 25 MINUTES

SERVES 4

2 tablespoons olive oil

4 large onions, thinly sliced

2 tablespoons white wine vinegar

2 tablespoons light brown sugar

Salt and pepper

All-purpose flour, for sprinkling

1 pound frozen puff pastry dough, defrosted

1$\frac{1}{4}$ cups grated cheddar cheese

Beaten egg or milk, to glaze

Green salad, to serve

1 Preheat the oven to 400°F. Heat the olive oil in a large frying pan. Add the sliced onions and sauté for about 10 minutes, stirring occasionally, until they are soft. Stir in the white wine vinegar and the sugar. Increase the heat and cook, stirring frequently, for 4 to 5 minutes longer, until the onions turn a deep caramel color. Season with salt and pepper; set aside to cool slightly.

2 On a lightly floured surface, roll out the dough into a 14 inch circle. Transfer it to a cookie sheet. Sprinkle half the grated cheddar over the dough, leaving a 2$\frac{1}{2}$-inch border around the edge. Spoon the caramelized onions over the cheese.

3 Fold the uncovered dough edges over the filling; aim for a homemade, rustic look. Brush the rim with beaten egg or milk. Sprinkle the remaining cheese over the dough and a little over the onions.

4 Bake for 20 to 25 minutes, until the pastry is puffy and golden. Serve cut into wedges with a green salad.

Spinach and Gruyère Tart

This is a quick-and-easy way of making a tart if you don't have a suitable tart or quiche pan.

If you don't have any pesto sauce, spread the dough with black olive paste or sun-dried tomato paste instead. If you want to use frozen spinach you will need only $\frac{1}{2}$ pound, and make sure it is leaf spinach, rather than chopped. It should also be thoroughly defrosted. Squeeze out the excess moisture before using, or your pastry will become soggy.

PREPARATION: 10 MINUTES

BAKING: 15 TO 20 MINUTES

SERVES 4

1 tablespoon sunflower oil

1 red onion, finely chopped

1 pound fresh spinach

Pastry dough for single pie crust, defrosted if frozen

2 tablespoons pesto sauce

1 cup grated Gruyère cheese

1 egg, beaten

Salt and pepper

1 Preheat the oven to 400°F. Heat the oil in a small pan. Add the chopped onion and sauté for 4 minutes until soft; remove from the heat. Place the spinach in a large pan with only the water from washing it that remains clinging to its leaves. Heat slowly until just wilted. Leave to cool, then squeeze out excess moisture.

2 Roll out the dough into a circle about 10 inches in diameter and place on a greased cookie sheet. Spread the dough with the pesto sauce. Stir the cheese (reserving 1 tablespoon), red onion, egg, and plenty of seasoning into the spinach. Place in the middle of the dough, leaving a 1$\frac{1}{4}$-inch border.

3 Fold the dough up around the spinach mixture and pinch the edges together to hold it in place. Sprinkle the reserved grated cheese over. Bake for 15 to 20 minutes until golden.

Tomato Tarte Tatin

Though it looks distinctly impressive, this tart is surprisingly easy to make.

PREPARATION: 20 MINUTES

BAKING: 15 TO 20 MINUTES, PLUS 5 MINUTES COOLING

SERVES 4

1 teaspoon olive oil

Large chunk butter

1 teaspoon sugar

9 to 10 tomatoes, halved crosswise

Salt and pepper

Green salad, to serve

FOR THE DOUGH:

$^2/_3$ cup all-purpose flour

4 tablespoons butter, diced

$^1/_2$ cup grated sharp cheddar cheese

4 scallions, chopped

Pinch salt

1 First make the dough: Process the flour, butter, and cheese in a food processor until you have the texture of coarse crumbs. Add the scallions and salt, and mix briefly. With the machine still running, add 2 to 3 tablespoons chilled water and process until the dough forms a ball. Wrap in plastic wrap.

2 In a $8^1/_2$- to 9-inch skillet, heat the oil and butter. Add the sugar and heat until caramelized, stirring it into the butter and oil. Pack the tomatoes into the pan, some cut-side up, some cut-side down, and season well. Cook over high heat for a few minutes until the tomatoes start to color on the undersides. Remove from the heat and leave to cool.

3 Preheat the oven to 400°F. Roll out the dough on a lightly floured surface until it is slightly larger than the pan. Put the dough over the tomatoes and tuck the edges down the sides. Bake for 15 to 20 minutes, until the pastry is golden. Remove from the heat and leave to cool for about 5 minutes so the juices can settle. Invert onto a plate so the pastry is on the bottom. Serve with a green salad.

Shallot Tatin

Pearl onions work just as well as the shallots.

PREPARATION: 45 MINUTES

BAKING: 20 TO 25 MINUTES

SERVES 4

$2^1/_4$ pounds shallots, peeled

2 tablespoons butter

1 tablespoon olive oil

1 teaspoon cumin seeds

3 tablespoons dark Barbados or raw sugar

Grated zest of $^1/_2$ lemon

Salt and pepper

FOR THE DOUGH:

$1^1/_3$ cups all-purpose flour

Pinch salt

$^1/_2$ cup butter, diced

1 egg yolk

$^1/_2$ cup finely chopped walnut pieces

1 Preheat the oven to 400°F. Make the dough: Place the flour, salt, butter, and egg yolk in a bowl. Using your fingertips, mix the fat and egg into the flour until mixture has the texture of coarse crumbs. Stir in the nuts and 2 to 3 tablespoons water– enough to form a smooth, firm dough. Knead briefly, shape into a ball, wrap in plastic wrap, and chill while preparing filling.

2 Bring a pan of water to a boil. Add the shallots and cook for 5 minutes. Drain and pat dry. Heat the butter and oil in a 9 to 10 inch skillet with a flameproof handle. Add the shallots and sauté, stirring, for about 10 minutes until they start to turn golden. Sprinkle on the cumin seeds, sugar, lemon zest, about 4 tablespoons of water, and seasoning. Cook for 5 minutes longer, until the shallots are soft and golden with a syrupy sauce; remove from the heat.

3 Roll out the dough on a floured surface to a circle about 2 inches larger than the pan. Supporting the dough with the rolling pin, place it over the shallots, tucking the edges down the side of pan. Bake for 20 to 25 minutes until the pastry is crisp and golden.

4 Let the tart cool in pan for 5 minutes. Place a large serving plate over it and invert the tart onto it, shallots on top. Serve warm, cut into wedges.

The Jerusalem artichoke—a relative of the sunflower—is generally a very underrated vegetable. Raw, the knobby tuber has a sweet, nutty flavor and can be shredded into salads, but it is more usually boiled, steamed, braised with butter, deep-fried in batter, or roasted. The tubers are notoriously difficult to peel, so they are often simply scrubbed or peeled after preliminary parboiling. If you do peel them raw, add some lemon juice to the soaking water, because otherwise they will discolor rapidly.

Jerusalem artichokes are among the most nourishing of winter root vegetables, rich in vitamin C and minerals such as potassium and phosphorus. The flavor is like that of the globe artichoke, so they make the most magnificent soups and purees. Buy unbruised specimens with as regular a shape as possible, because they are the easiest to prepare.

Jerusalem artichokes

Jerusalem Artichoke and Mushroom Dauphinoise

1 Preheat the oven to 350°F. Cook 1 1/2 pounds Jerusalem artichokes in lightly salted, boiling water for 7 to 10 minutes, until just tender.

2 Meanwhile, heat 2 tablespoons olive oil in a large pan. Add 1 sliced onion and 2 crushed garlic cloves and sauté for 3 minutes until soft. Increase the heat. Add 5 cups sliced crimini mushrooms and cook for 5 to 6 minutes longer, tossing occasionally, until golden.

3 Drain the artichokes and refresh under cold running water. Drain again and peel. Cut any large artichokes in half and arrange in a shallow 1 1/4-quart dish with the mushroom mixture.

4 In a bowl, mix together 3/4 cup plus 2 tablespoons crème fraîche or sour cream, 2/3 cup light cream, 1 tablespoon whole-grain mustard, a pinch of grated nutmeg, the grated zest of 1 lemon, and 1 tablespoon chopped fresh parsley. Season and pour over the vegetables.

5 Sprinkle 1/2 cup grated Gruyère cheese over the top. Bake for 30 to 35 minutes until golden. Serve immediately.

Leek, Ham, and Camembert Gratin

Camembert melts really well for this dish, but other types of cheese work, too. If you don't have Camembert, use crumbled Stilton, grated Gruyère, or even sharp cheddar instead—each of these adds its own distinctive flavor.

PREPARATION: 20 MINUTES
COOKING: ABOUT 25 MINUTES
SERVES 4

2¹/₂ cups chicken or vegetable stock
1¹/₂ pounds scrubbed, unpeeled potatoes, thickly sliced
3¹/₂ cups sliced leeks
4 ounces wafer-thin slices ham
Salt and pepper
4¹/₂ ounces Camembert cheese, thinly sliced
Broccoli or green beans, to serve

1 In a large pan, bring the stock to a boil. Add the potatoes and cook for 15 minutes until just tender, adding the leeks for the last 5 minutes of cooking time. Drain, reserving 4 tablespoons of the stock.
2 Preheat the broiler. Layer the sliced potatoes and leeks with the ham in a shallow gratin dish and season with salt and pepper between the layers. Pour the reserved stock over. 3 Lay the cheese on top. Broil for 5 minutes until the cheese has melted and is beginning to brown.
4 Serve immediately with broccoli or green beans.

VARIATIONS: For a richer gratin, pour ³/₄ cup plus 2 tablespoons crème fraîche or sour cream over the layers instead of the stock. You can also add a crushed garlic clove or two to the crème fraîche if you like. If you prefer, you can also bake the dish in a 350°F oven for 20 to 25 minutes.

Carrot and Potato Flat Bread

PREPARATION: 25 MINUTES
BAKING: 35 TO 40 MINUTES
SERVES 12

Butter, for greasing
1 pound new potatoes, scrubbed
1 egg
1¹/₄ cups 2% milk
2 tablespoons chopped fresh rosemary
3 small carrots, grated
Generous ³/₄ cup rice flour
Generous ³/₄ cup potato flour
2 tablespoons soy flour
1 teaspoon baking soda
¹/₂ teaspoon cream of tartar
¹/₂ teaspoon coarse sea salt
Salt and pepper

1 Preheat the oven to 425°F. Grease a 13 × 9-inch baking pan and line it with waxed paper. Cook the potatoes in boiling, salted water for 8 to 10 minutes until tender. Drain, leave to cool, and slice.
2 Beat the egg and milk together. Stir half of the rosemary into the egg mixture and add the grated carrots.
3 In a separate bowl, combine the dry ingredients, except the remaining rosemary and sea salt. Fold into the egg mixture. Season to taste.
4 Pour the batter into the prepared pan. Arrange the sliced potatoes on top and sprinkle with the remaining rosemary and the salt.
5 Bake for 35 to 40 minutes, until a skewer inserted into the bread comes out clean.

Polenta, Red Pepper, and Zucchini Gratin

If you've never used polenta, you'll be surprised how easy it is to cook with and how well it complements the flavor of the broiled vegetables.

PREPARATION: 50 MINUTES
COOKING: 20 TO 30 MINUTES
SERVES 4

1 tablespoon butter, plus more for greasing

2 red bell peppers

3 tablespoons olive oil

2 eggplants, thickly sliced

2 large zucchini, sliced lengthwise

2 garlic cloves, minced

5$\frac{1}{2}$ ounces fresh mozzarella cheese, drained and sliced

2$\frac{1}{2}$ cups vegetable stock

$\frac{2}{3}$ cup quick-cooking polenta

$\frac{3}{4}$ cup grated Gruyère cheese

2 tablespoons chopped fresh thyme, or 2 teaspoons dried

Salt and pepper

1 Preheat the oven to 400°F and preheat the broiler to high. Butter a 1$\frac{1}{2}$-quart shallow gratin dish; set aside. Place the peppers under the broiler and broil for 5 to 7 minutes, turning occasionally, until black all over. Seal in a paper bag; set aside to cool.

2 Brush oil over the eggplant and zucchini slices. Broil for 3 to 4 minutes on each side until lightly brown. When the peppers are cool, halve them and remove the skin, core, and seeds. Slice the flesh. Place all the vegetables in the prepared dish, scatter the garlic over, and top with the mozzarella.

3 In a large pan, bring the stock to a boil. Add the polenta in a steady stream and cook for 3 to 4 minutes, stirring constantly, until thick and starting to come away from the sides of the pan.

4 Off the heat, stir in half the Gruyère, the 1 tablespoon butter, and the thyme; season well. Spoon the polenta over the mozzarella. Sprinkle the remaining Gruyère over. Bake for 20 to 30 minutes, until the top has a rich, golden color.

Tian of Zucchini

This dish is a favorite with almost everyone because it is very filling. It can also be served cold with salads and is ideal for taking on picnics.

PREPARATION: 35 MINUTES

BAKING: 45 MINUTES

SERVES 8

2 tablespoons butter, plus more for greasing

4 tablespoons olive oil

$3^1/_2$ cups trimmed and chopped leeks

3 garlic cloves, minced

$7^1/_2$ cups trimmed and diced zucchini

18 ounces frozen spinach, defrosted and drained

$^3/_4$ cup brown rice, cooked according to package directions

5 large eggs, beaten

$2^1/_4$ cups grated Gruyère cheese

Salt and pepper

$^1/_2$ cup grated Parmesan cheese

1 cup fresh breadcrumbs

1 Preheat the oven to 350°F. Lightly butter the bottom and sides of a medium-sized shallow gratin dish.

2 Heat the oil in a large pan. Add the leeks and sauté over low heat for 5 to 6 minutes, stirring occasionally, until soft. Add the garlic and zucchini and cook for 10 minutes longer until tender, turning the vegetables over occasionally.

3 Remove the vegetables from the heat and stir in the spinach, cooked rice, eggs, and Gruyère, stirring well to combine; season generously. Spread the mixture into the prepared dish and sprinkle the Parmesan and breadcrumbs evenly over the top. Dot with the 2 tablespoons butter.

4 Bake for 45 minutes, until the top is golden and the mixture is lightly set.

Polenta-Squash Layer

PREPARATION: 45 MINUTES

BAKING: 35 TO 40 MINUTES

SERVES 4

3 cups vegetable stock (see page 17)

$1^1/_2$ cups quick-cooking polenta

5 tablespoons grated Parmesan cheese

7 tablespoons butter

Salt and pepper

1 small butternut squash, about 18 ounces peeled, seeded, and chopped

1 small onion, chopped

2 garlic cloves, crushed

$1^1/_2$ cups sliced button mushrooms

$5^1/_2$ ounces fresh spinach, stems removed

2 fresh sage leaves, chopped

$^3/_4$ cup ricotta cheese

1 Line a 15 × 10-inch baking dish with plastic wrap. Put the stock in a large pan and bring to a rolling boil. Drizzle in the polenta and cook, stirring constantly, for 3 to 4 minutes, until thick and coming away from the side. Off the heat, beat in half the Parmesan and half the butter until smooth. Season and spoon into the prepared pan, spreading into all the corners; leave to cool.

2 Preheat the oven to 375°F. Cook the butternut squash in a pan of lightly salted boiling water for 6 to 8 minutes, until tender; drain.

3 Meanwhile, heat the remaining butter in a large pan. Add the onion and garlic and sauté for 3 to 4 minutes, stirring occasionally, until slightly soft. Stir in the mushrooms and cook for 10 minutes, stirring occasionally. Stir in the spinach, cover, and simmer for 2 minutes. Stir in the squash, sage, and seasoning to taste.

4 Cut the polenta into 12 rectangles. Spread the ricotta cheese over 8 of these rectangles; season. Place 4 of these rectangles, cheese-side up, on a lightly greased baking tray and spread them with half the mushroom mixture, then top each with another cheese-topped rectangle and more mushroom mixture. Top with a plain piece of polenta. Sprinkle the remaining Parmesan over. Bake for 35 to 40 minutes, until golden.

Creamy Mushroom Lasagna

This recipe uses crimini and white mushrooms, but it is a versatile dish, and you could use any combination of mushrooms you have available.

PREPARATION: 30 MINUTES

BAKING: 30 MINUTES

SERVES 4

2 tablespoons butter

8¹⁄₂ cups thinly sliced mixed mushrooms,
   such as crimini and white

2 garlic cloves, crushed

9 ounces fresh lasagna noodles

²⁄₃ cup heavy cream

Grated zest of 1 lemon

1 cup plus 2 tablespoons ricotta cheese

Salt and pepper

Vegetable oil for greasing

4 tablespoons chopped fresh parsley

10 ounces fresh mozzarella cheese, drained
   and thinly sliced

4 tablespoons freshly grated Parmesan cheese

1 Preheat the oven to 425°F. Melt the butter in a large skillet. Add the sliced mushrooms and crushed garlic and sauté slowly for 5 to 8 minutes, until soft.
2 Put the pasta into a large bowl and cover with boiling water; set aside for 5 minutes.
3 Pour the cream into a small pan and heat slowly. Stir in the lemon zest and simmer for 2 to 3 minutes. Carefully stir in the ricotta cheese. Heat through and season well.
4 Drain the pasta well. In a greased baking dish, layer the lasagna, ricotta mixture, garlic and mushrooms, parsley, mozzarella, and Parmesan. Continue these layers, finishing with the lasagna, a little sauce, some mozzarella, and a sprinkling of Parmesan. (If you like, the dish can be prepared ahead up to this point and refrigerated overnight.)
5 Bake for 30 minutes, until the pasta is tender and the top is bubbling and golden brown.

Vegetable Lasagna

This recipe may look long and complicated, but it isn't. This is one of those curious dishes that are much more difficult to explain than they are actually to make.

PREPARATION: 50 MINUTES

BAKING: 55 TO 60 MINUTES

SERVES 6

1 eggplant

3 zucchini

3 tablespoons olive oil

Salt and pepper

3 red or yellow bell peppers

$^{1}/_{2}$ pound cooked lasagna noodles

4 tablespoons chopped fresh parsley

$^{1}/_{2}$ cup grated Parmesan cheese

6 ounces fresh mozzarella cheese,
   thinly sliced

FOR THE TOMATO SAUCE:

2 tablespoons olive oil

1 onion, minced

2 garlic cloves, crushed

1 carrot, grated

2 (14 ounce) cans crushed tomatoes

Salt and pepper

$^{2}/_{3}$ cup red wine (optional)

Handful fresh basil leaves

FOR THE BÉCHAMEL SAUCE:

4 tablespoons butter

5 tablespoons all-purpose flour

$2^{1}/_{2}$ cups 2% milk

Pinch freshly grated nutmeg

1 First make the tomato sauce. Heat the oil in a large, heavy-bottomed pan. Add the onion and garlic and sauté for 3 minutes, until soft. Stir in the carrot and cook for 2 minutes longer. Add the tomatoes and wine and season to taste. Simmer for 25 to 30 minutes, until the sauce is thick and reduced. Stir in the basil; set aside.

2 Preheat the oven to 425°F. Cut the eggplant and zucchini lengthwise into $^{1}/_{4}$-inch slices. Brush with some olive oil, sprinkle with a little salt, and place on a baking sheet. Bake for 15 to 20 minutes, until brown and soft. At the same time, bake the peppers whole for 15 to 20 minutes, until the skins are lightly charred and wrinkled. After removing them from the oven, place the peppers in a paper bag until completely cool. Halve them, remove skin and seeds, and cut the flesh into wide strips.

3 To make the béchamel sauce, first melt the butter in a heavy-bottomed saucepan. Then stir in the flour and cook, stirring, over low heat. Remove from the heat and gradually pour in the milk, stirring constantly with a balloon whisk or wooden spoon. Return to the heat and continue stirring for about 5 minutes until the sauce thickens. Stir in the nutmeg and season well. Remove from the heat; set aside.

4 To assemble the lasagna, spoon about half of the tomato sauce into the bottom of a 8 × 10-inch lasagna dish. Arrange about one-third of the lasagna noodles in a single layer on top.

5 Cover the lasagna with half of the eggplant and sprinkle with a little parsley. Add half the peppers and zucchini. Spoon one-third of the béchamel sauce on top and sprinkle with one-third of the Parmesan and mozzarella cheese.

6 Repeat with another third of the pasta, the remaining tomato sauce and vegetables, and another third of the béchamel sauce and cheeses. Finally, top with the remaining pasta, béchamel sauce, and cheeses.

7 Cover with foil and bake for 25 to 30 minutes. Remove the foil and bake for 10 minutes longer until golden brown and bubbling.

The cabbage is one of the most ancient of cultivated vegetables, dating back more than four thousand years. The Celts are believed to have brought it to Europe from Asia before it traveled to North America. Its ability to thrive in cold climates made it a popular crop.

Cabbage can be fabulous or foul, depending on how it is cooked. Properly cooked, it retains its crunch, flavor, and copious nutrients; overcooked, it loses them all and produces the depressingly pervasive sulfurous odor so redolent of institutional cooking. When boiling cabbage, to keep the crispness and color, cook for just 5 to 7 minutes.

Buy only cabbages with firm but tender, unblemished leaves that are neither withered nor puffy; the denser-hearted winter varieties, like the Savoy and red cabbages, should be firm and solid in their centers and weigh heavy for their size. Buy only those with their loose outer leaves still in place, because these are good indicators of freshness and also help protect the inner leaves.

Don't forget that raw cabbage makes the ideal winter substitute for lettuce in salads. Shred it finely and dress it with mustard- or nut-flavored dressing.

Cabbage

Sausage-Stuffed Cabbage

1 Preheat the oven to 325°F. Bring a large pan of salted water to a boil. Pull any coarse leaves off the outside of a Savoy cabbage and trim the bottom so it stands upright. Carve out the core from below—the hard woody bit—but keep the whole intact.

2 Plunge the cabbage into the pan of boiling water and boil for precisely 5 minutes; drain and set aside to cool. Meanwhile, mix 1 pound best-quality sausage meat, 1 beaten egg, and seasoning in a bowl.

3 When the cabbage is cool enough to handle, slowly peel back all the leaves like a flower. Stop when you get to the tiny leaves in the middle.

4 Put 1 tablespoon of the sausage meat at the bottom of the last leaf pulled back. Continue, gradually reassembling the cabbage and holding it in shape as you do. Keep the filling to the bottom of each leaf—it shouldn't squeeze out.

5 Tie the cabbage into shape. Put a piece of string around the middle and tie in place, then tie other pieces around the cabbage at intervals until it feels secure.

6 Put in a large pot with $2^{1}/_{2}$ cups sauce or chicken stock and white wine and cover with a little lightly buttered foil and a tight-fitting lid. Bake for 3 to 4 hours until meltingly tender.

7 Remove the string and slice the stuffed cabbage as you would a cake.

Cabbage Rolls with Roasted Ratatouille

PREPARATION: 25 MINUTES

BAKING: 40 MINUTES

SERVES 4

2 onions, cut into wedges

2 large eggplants, roughly chopped

8 tomatoes, quartered

4 tablespoons olive oil

1 cup long-grain rice

8 herb-flavored sausage links

2 red bell peppers, seeded, cored, and
    chopped

2 tablespoons chopped fresh parsley

1 1/2 cups grated sharp cheddar cheese

8 Savoy cabbage lettuce leaves, thick veins
    removed

Salt and freshly ground black pepper

1 Preheat the oven to 375°F. Put the onions, eggplants, and tomatoes in a roasting pan, drizzle with oil, and season to taste. Bake for 30 minutes until the vegetables start to brown.

2 Meanwhile, cook the rice in boiling, salted water until tender; drain. Fry the sausages in a nonstick skillet for 8 to 10 minutes, turning occasionally, until brown and cooked; remove from the pan. Add the peppers to the pan and cook for 4 to 5 minutes, stirring occasionally, until soft. Chop the sausages and stir into the pan with the parsley, rice, and cheese; season.

3 Blanch the cabbage leaves in boiling salted water for 2 minutes. Drain and pat dry. Spoon some rice into the middle of each leaf. Roll up and tuck in the ends.

4 Sit the cabbage rolls on top of the vegetables, seams down. Heat in the oven for 10 minutes. Cut each cabbage roll in half before serving.

Roasted Stuffed Onions

PREPARATION: 15 MINUTES

ROASTING: 1 HOUR 20 MINUTES

SERVES 4

4 large onions, sliced into quarters but
   with the roots left intact

2 tablespoons olive oil

Salt and pepper

2 large potatoes, grated

2 large carrots, grated

3 tablespoons whole-grain mustard

2 tablespoons butter

$^3/_4$ cup grated Gruyère cheese

1 Preheat the oven to 400°F. Place the onions on a baking tray, brush with the olive oil, and season. Roast for about 1 hour until golden and tender.

2 Meanwhile, mix the potato and carrot together. Stir in the mustard and seasoning. Divide the mixture among the onions and dot the top of each with the butter.

3 Return the onions to the oven and roast for 15 minutes longer, until they are meltingly tender.

4 Sprinkle with the Gruyère cheese and roast for 5 minutes longer, until the toppings are golden and bubbling.

Roasted Squash with Lime and Caper Sauce

Deep-fried capers are a revelation—nutty, crisp, and capery all in one. Sizzle them up in a little oil at the last minute to serve them at their best. Serve this dish as a light lunch or as an accompaniment to broiled meat.

PREPARATION: 20 MINUTES

ROASTING: 40 MINUTES

SERVES 4

1 kabocha or other winter squash, or wedge of
   pumpkin, 2 to 3 pounds in weight

6 garlic cloves, unpeeled

2 tablespoons sunflower oil or light olive oil

2 sprigs fresh thyme or lemon thyme

2 bay leaves

1 sprig rosemary

FOR THE LIME AND CAPER SAUCE:

$^2/_3$ cup plain yogurt

Juice of 1 lime

1 heaped tablespoon large capers, rinsed and
   soaked if salted, chopped

FOR THE FRIED CAPERS:

Sunflower oil

2 heaped tablespoons capers, rinsed and
   soaked if salted, dried thoroughly

1 Preheat the oven to 400°F. Cut the squash into 1- to 1$^1/_2$-inch wedges; discard the seeds, but leave the skin on. Put in a roasting pan with the garlic, oil, and herbs and stir to coat the squash and garlic in the oil. Roast for 40 minutes, turning once or twice, until the squash is tender.

2 Make the Lime and Caper Sauce by mixing together all the ingredients.

3 Fry the capers: Heat enough sunflower oil to fill a small pan to a depth of about $^1/_2$ inch until a bread cube browns in it in 20 seconds. Test a couple of capers by frying them for 10 seconds if small, 15 seconds if large. Lift out and drain on paper towels; they should be crisp and retain some color. If black or bitter, reduce the heat and try again.

4 Divide the squash among 4 plates or bowls. Drizzle with a little sauce and scatter with fried capers. Serve the rest of the sauce separately.

The Mediterranean diet has always made the most of an abundance of sun-ripened vegetables, enhanced by the warmth of Mediterranean flavorings like olives and olive oil, garlic, pine nuts, basil, and oregano. They are used to make a diverse range of pasta sauces, in glorious multicolored toppings for pizzas and in the most tempting of creamy risottos.

Make it Mediterranean

Pasta, Pizza, Risotto, etc.

Pasta with Broccoli and Toasted Nuts

Instead of Camembert, you can crumble in blue cheese or feta, or simply shave Parmesan over the top.

PREPARATION: ABOUT 15 MINUTES
COOKING: 15 TO 20 MINUTES
SERVES 2 (EASILY DOUBLED)

6 ounces spaghetti
Salt and pepper
1^1/$_2$ cups broccoli, cut into small florets
Olive oil for frying and dressing
^{1}/$_2$ cup mixed chopped nuts
1 garlic clove, minced
3 tablespoons chopped fresh parsley
Grated zest and juice of 1 small lemon
4 ounces Camembert or brie, cut into
    small pieces

1 Cook the pasta in lots of rapidly boiling salted water until just tender. Add the broccoli for the last 3 minutes of cooking time.
2 Heat a little olive oil in a small pan. Add the nuts and cook until lightly toasted, stirring frequently. Add the garlic and cook for about 20 seconds, until just brown. Remove from the heat and stir in the parsley and lemon zest.
3 Drain the pasta and broccoli. Return them to the pan and stir in the nut mixture and cheese. Season well.
4 Drizzle with olive oil and lemon juice to serve.

Cheesy Spaghetti with Zucchini and Bacon

This simple, easy-to-do baked pasta dish is a great way of getting children to eat greens—and tastes really delicious, too.

PREPARATION: 20 MINUTES
BAKING: 20 TO 25 MINUTES
SERVES 4

12 ounces spaghetti
Salt and pepper
2 tablespoons butter, plus more for the dish
1 onion, minced
8 slices smoked bacon, cut into small strips
2 tablespoons all-purpose flour
2^1/$_2$ cups milk
1^1/$_2$ cups zucchini cut into
    matchstick strips
2 cups finely grated sharp cheddar cheese
2 rounded tablespoons whole grain mustard

1 Preheat the oven to 425°F. Cook the spaghetti in lots of rapidly boiling salted water until just al dente.
2 Meanwhile, melt the butter in a pan. Add the onion and bacon, and fry for 5 minutes until soft and golden. Sprinkle the flour over and cook for 1 minute, stirring. Gradually add the milk, stirring to make a thick smooth sauce.
3 Bring the sauce to a boil. Add the zucchini and simmer for a couple of minutes. Remove from the heat and stir in all but a handful of the cheese and all the mustard. Season.
4 Drain the pasta well and mix with the cheese sauce. Spoon the mixture into a large, buttered baking dish and scatter the reserved cheese over. Bake for 20 to 25 minutes until bubbling and golden brown.

Spaghetti alla Puttanesca

The name of this traditional Italian dish translates literally as "prostitute's spaghetti."

PREPARATION: 10 TO 15 MINUTES
COOKING: 10 TO 12 MINUTES
SERVES 3 TO 4

1 pound spaghetti

4 tablespoons olive oil

1 (14 ounce) can crushed tomatoes

1 red chile, seeded and finely chopped

8 canned anchovy fillets, drained and chopped

2 garlic cloves, chopped

2 tablespoons butter

Scant 1 cup sliced, pitted ripe olives

2 tablespoons small capers, rinsed and soaked if salted

4 tablespoons chopped fresh parsley

Salt and pepper

1 Cook the pasta in lots of rapidly boiling salted water.
2 Heat 1 tablespoon of the oil in a pan. Add the tomatoes. Bring to a boil and cook for 4 to 5 minutes, stirring and crushing them with a wooden spoon.
3 Sauté the chile, anchovies, and garlic in the remaining oil and the butter for 1 to 2 minutes, mashing the anchovies.
4 Add the tomatoes, olives, and capers. Cook for 2 to 3 minutes, stirring.
5 Drain the pasta when it is just al dente. Add to the sauce. Sprinkle the parsley and some seasoning over. Stir well before serving.

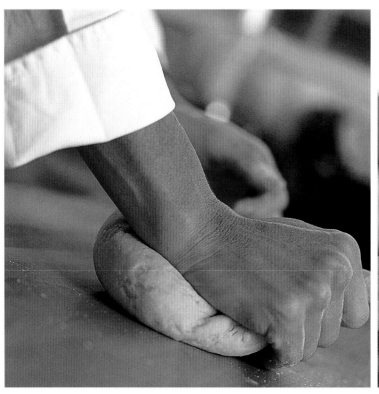

Fennel Raviolini

Homemade pasta is easier to make than you may think. For the best results, weigh the flour and use Italian "00" flour, a very fine-textured wheat flour traditionally used in Italy; it is available from some mail order and specialty food stores. If you can't find it, use bread flour instead. Semolina flour helps the pasta to dry. It also helps give the recipe an authentic Italian flavor, as well as its wonderful yellow color.

PREPARATION: 40 MINUTES
PLUS CHILLING AND
RESTING
MAKES 54 RAVIOLINI

FOR THE PASTA:
4 ounces "00" flour (1 cup sifted flour)
4 ounces grano duro di semolo
  (semolina flour) (1 cup sifted flour)
2 large eggs
2 teaspoons fine sea salt
1 tablespoon extra-virgin olive oil

1 First make the pasta: Open all the windows to cool the kitchen and rinse your hands in cold water. Sift the flours into a mound on a clean countertop and make a well in the center. Break in the eggs and add the salt and olive oil. Beat the eggs lightly with a fork, and draw in the flour without allowing any egg to escape, until you have a rough-textured dough.

2 Use your hands to bring the rough dough into a smooth ball. Discard any crusty flour and knead the dough on the countertop, adding a little more "00" flour if necessary, for 8 to 10 minutes, until the dough is silky smooth. Wrap in plastic wrap and chill for 20 minutes.

3 Meanwhile, make the filling. Lightly steam the minced fennel for 5 minutes over a pan of simmering water; leave to cool slightly. Beat with

FOR THE FILLING:

1 small fennel bulb, minced

1 cup ricotta cheese

$^1/_4$ cup fresh basil leaves,
    shredded

$^1/_2$ cup grated Parmesan cheese plus extra
    shavings to serve

the ricotta cheese, fresh basil, and freshly grated Parmesan. Season to taste.

4 Remove the dough from the refrigerator; it should now be smooth and marbled. Cut off one-eighth of the dough, wrap the rest in plastic wrap, and return it to the refrigerator. Roll out the piece of dough on a lightly floured surface to flatten it slightly until it measures about 8 × 3 inches.

5 Adjust the pasta machine to the thickest setting. Sprinkle semolina flour over the rollers to stop the dough from sticking. Roll the dough through the machine. Repeat, then move machine on to the next setting and roll the dough through in a continuous motion, twice. Repeat until you reach the second thinnest setting. (Many experts never put the pasta through on the final setting because they find it often tears.) Lay the strip on a work surface and leave to rest for 8 to 10 minutes. Repeat with the remaining dough.

6 Use a 3-inch fluted cutter to cut out about 54 pasta circles. Spoon $^3/_4$ teaspoon of filling into the middle of each circle of dough. Brush the edge with a little water, fold each circle over in half, and pinch the edges together to seal.

7 Arrange the finished raviolini on a wire rack and leave to dry for at least 15 minutes. (If you aren't going to use the pasta immediately, transfer to the freezer at this stage; it can be frozen for up to 3 months.) Keep the leftover dough and cut into small pieces and dry with the rest of the pasta. These can then be added to soup as a thickener.

Fennel Raviolini with Roasted Vegetable and Saffron Sauce

PREPARATION: 15 MINUTES
ROASTING: 25 MINUTES
SERVES 6

Fennel raviolini (see pages 94–95)
2 fennel bulbs, trimmed and sliced
4 small red onions, cut into wedges
5 tablespoons extra-virgin olive oil
Salt and pepper
1 garlic clove, minced
2 shallots, minced
Large pinch saffron threads
1 cup plus 2 tablespoons dry white wine
1 1/2 cups mascarpone cheese
Fresh basil and flat-leaf parsley, to serve

1 To prepare the roasted vegetables and saffron sauce; preheat the oven to 375°F. Place the fennel and onions on a large baking tray and drizzle 4 tablespoons of the olive oil over. Season and roast for 25 minutes, until the vegetables are just beginning to char.
2 Meanwhile, heat the remaining olive oil in a pan. Add the garlic and shallots, and sweat for 5 minutes over low heat until soft. Stir in the saffron and wine. Bring to a boil and simmer until reduced by half.
3 Stir in the mascarpone cheese and beat the mixture until smooth. Cook over low heat, stirring, for 5 minutes. The more you cook the sauce, the more yellow it will become, because the saffron gradually infuses into the mixture.
4 Bring a large pan of lightly salted water to a boil. Add the stuffed pasta, return to a boil, and cook for 3 to 4 minutes (frozen pasta will take 5 to 6 minutes). Drain and toss with the roasted vegetables and saffron sauce. Serve sprinkled with the Parmesan shavings and fresh herbs.

Fiorelli with Oven-Dried Vegetables and Tapenade

PREPARATION: 15 MINUTES
ROASTING: 1 HOUR
SERVES 4

2 or 3 zucchini, cut into thick slices at an angle
8 ounces cherry tomatoes, halved and pulp and
    seeds removed
Salt and pepper
1 tablespoon sugar
2 tablespoons olive oil
12 ounces dried fiorelli (pasta trumpets)
Mixed fresh herbs, to garnish (optional)
Freshly grated Parmesan cheese, to serve
FOR THE TAPENADE:
1 1/2 cups pitted ripe olives
1 tablespoon capers, drained
1 large garlic clove
1 teaspoon lemon juice
5 tablespoons extra-virgin olive oil

1 To prepare the oven-dried vegetables, preheat the oven to 300°F. Place the zucchini slices and tomato halves on a large baking tray and sprinkle with a little salt and sugar. Drizzle the olive oil over. Roast for about 1 hour, turning the tray from time to time so the vegetables receive even heat.
2 Meanwhile, make the tapenade. Put the olives, capers, garlic, lemon juice, and olive oil in a food processor and process to a paste.
3 Bring a large pan of salted water to a boil. Add the pasta. Bring back to a good rolling boil and cook until just al dente, about 5 to 6 minutes; drain.
4 Stir the tapenade into the pasta and toss with the oven-dried vegetables. Garnish with herbs, if you like, and serve with the Parmesan.

Char-grilled Vegetable Pasticcio

PREPARATION: 50 MINUTES
BAKING: 30 MINUTES
SERVES 8

3 red and 3 yellow bell peppers, seeded and quartered
2 large eggplants, thinly sliced lengthwise
3 tablespoons olive oil
1 pound tagliatelle
2 tablespoons butter
1 small onion, minced
2 garlic cloves, crushed
6 tablespoons white wine or dry vermouth
1¼ cups heavy cream
1½ cups finely grated Gruyère cheese
Salt and pepper
2 eggs, lightly beaten

1 Preheat the broiler to high and the oven to 375°F. Broil the peppers, skin-side up, for 5 to 6 minutes, until the skin is black and blistered. Place in a plastic bag and leave to steam for about 5 minutes, so the skins will loosen.
2 Brush both sides of the eggplant slices with the olive oil and season. Heat a griddle or frying pan and fry the eggplant slices for 2 to 3 minutes on each side until scorched. Use to line a deep 9 inch, removable-bottom tart pan, overlapping the slices and letting them overhang the edge of the pan.
3 Cook the pasta until just tender. Meanwhile, melt the butter in a small pan, and sauté the onion and garlic for 2 to 3 minutes until soft. Stir in wine or vermouth and cream, and heat slowly until almost boiling. Remove from the heat and stir in the cheese. Season, leave to cool slightly, and stir in the eggs.
4 Drain the pasta, return to the pan, and mix in the sauce.
5 Peel the peppers. Spoon half the pasta into the eggplant-lined pan and level. Cover with the red peppers. Spoon the remaining pasta over and top with the yellow peppers. Fold the overhanging eggplant slices in over the filling.
6 Cover with buttered aluminum foil and bake for 30 minutes until firm. Leave to stand for a few minutes before turning out on a plate.

Spicy Pepper Penne

Chorizo gives this pasta dish a delightful spicy kick, but you can use the same quantity of thinly sliced salami if you prefer.

PREPARATION: 25 MINUTES
BAKING: 15 TO 20 MINUTES
SERVES 4

4 tablespoons olive oil
3 red bell peppers, seeded, cored and cut into ½-inch-wide strips
1 large onion, thinly sliced
2 garlic cloves, crushed
2 (14 ounce) cans crushed tomatoes
Salt and pepper
10 ounces penne or rigatoni
5 ounces chorizo, sliced
Butter for greasing
1 slice white bread, made into crumbs
2 tablespoons chopped fresh rosemary, or 2 teaspoons dried
¼ cup freshly grated Parmesan cheese

1 Preheat the oven to 400°F. Heat 3 tablespoons of the oil in a pan and cook the peppers and onion for 10 minutes until soft and golden, shaking the pan occasionally. Stir in the garlic and cook for 1 minute. Add the tomatoes and heat through. Season.
2 Meanwhile, cook the pasta in lots of rapidly boiling salted water until just al dente. Drain well and mix it with the sauce and chorizo. Spoon the mixture into a buttered, large, shallow baking dish.
3 Mix together the breadcrumbs, rosemary, and Parmesan; sprinkle over the pasta. (You can make this dish ahead up to this point and chill overnight.)
4 Drizzle with the remaining oil. Bake for 15 to 20 minutes, until golden.

Marinated Couscous with Harissa Tomatoes

Harissa, a Moroccan chile paste, is available from some supermarkets and food stores. If you can't find any, stir chile sauce into 2 teaspoons tomato paste and use that instead.

PREPARATION: 10 MINUTES

COOKING: 15 MINUTES

SERVES 4

1 1/4 cups couscous

1 1/2 cups vegetable stock (see page 17)

4 sun-dried tomatoes in oil, drained and chopped

1/4 cup pitted ripe olives, quartered

1 tablespoon capers, drained

1/4 cup chopped fresh cilantro

Salt and pepper

FOR THE HARISSA TOMATOES:

1 tablespoon olive oil

2 teaspoons harissa

6 plum tomatoes, halved

1 1/2 ounces arugula

1 Place the couscous in a shallow dish and pour the stock over it. Leave to stand for 10 minutes until all the stock is absorbed.

2 Meanwhile, make the harissa tomatoes. Brush a large griddle or frying pan with 1 teaspoon of the oil and heat until smoking-hot. Mix the remaining oil with the harissa and spread over the cut sides of the tomatoes. Place, cut-side down, on the pan and cook for 2 minutes.

3 Fluff up the couscous with a fork. Stir the sun-dried tomatoes, olives, capers, and cilantro into the couscous and season.

4 Divide the couscous among 4 serving plates. Arrange the tomatoes over the couscous and top with the arugula. Serve.

Tomato and Mushroom Stacks

Ready-made polenta is sold in large sausage or oblong shapes and is not to be confused with quick-cook polenta, still in grain form.

PREPARATION: 20 MINUTES
ROASTING: ABOUT 30 MINUTES
SERVES 4

1 pound ready-made polenta (see above)

$1/2$ teaspoon dried oregano

$1/2$ cup freshly grated Parmesan cheese

1 cup freshly grated cheddar cheese

4 tablespoons olive oil

Salt and pepper

4 large flat mushrooms, stems removed

14 ounces tomatoes, roughly chopped

1 garlic clove, minced

1 Preheat the oven to 425°F. Cut the polenta in 12 slices about $1/2$ inch thick and stack these in 4 overlapping piles. Sprinkle with oregano and most of the cheeses.
2 Pour the oil into a bowl, season, and brush each mushroom with it. Place stem-side up on the polenta stacks.
3 Add the tomatoes and garlic to the remaining oil. Spoon the tomatoes and their juices in and around the mushrooms and polenta, then season with salt and pepper. Sprinkle over the remaining cheese.
4 Roast in the oven for about 30 minutes, until the tomatoes have softened and the mushrooms are tender. Serve hot.

Mozzarella Pasta with Olives and Chile

PREPARATION: 15 MINUTES
COOKING: ABOUT 15 MINUTES
SERVES 4

4 cups penne or rigatoni

Salt and pepper

1 small red onion, finely chopped

1 red chile, seeded and minced

1 pound ripe tomatoes, chopped

6 tablespoons olive oil

8 ounces fresh buffalo mozzarella, chopped

Handful of small fresh basil or mint leaves

$1/2$ cup black olives

1 Cook the pasta in a large pan of boiling salted water for 10 to 12 minutes until just al dente, stirring from time to time.
2 Meanwhile, in a large bowl, mix together the onion, chile, and tomatoes. Season with plenty of salt and pepper, then stir in the oil.
3 Drain the pasta and add it to the tomato mixture, together with the mozzarella, basil, and olives. Stir well and serve immediately.

VARIATION: This works best with authentic buffalo mozzarella; if you can't find that, however, rather than falling back on the bland blocks of cows'-milk substitute, try making the dish with another nice flavorful melting cheese, like fontina, or even cheddar.

Spinach is thought to have originated in Persia, where it was first cultivated for the delectation of cats, and was taken to Europe by the Moors in the sixteenth century. It is, therefore, unusual among our common vegetables in having been unknown to the ancient Romans. Catherine de Medici, who left her native Florence to marry King Henry II of France, is credited with having introduced it to the French court, hence all dishes containing spinach are referred to by the French as à la Florentine.

Spinach can be gritty, so soak the leaves for about an hour in cold water and then rinse them in several changes of fresh water, taking the leaves out to leave grit behind. The stems and any tough ribs should also be removed. The best way to cook the leaves is in a tightly covered pan with just the water left clinging to them after rinsing. Cooked spinach will absorb several times its own weight of melted butter and goes incredibly well with eggs and ham. Young leaves are also excellent raw in salads.

Although the leaves are highly nutritious, being notably rich in iron and vitamin A, the oxalic acid in spinach when cooked does not allow the abundance of nutrients to be absorbed by the body—so use the vegetable raw where you can.

Spinach

Roman Spinach

This simple treatment makes an excellent and characterful accompaniment to rich veal, poultry, and fish dishes.

1 Cram 1 pound cleaned and trimmed spinach leaves (see above) into a large pan. Cover and cook for 2 to 3 minutes, shaking the pan occasionally, until the leaves wilt. Drain in a colander.
2 Heat 2 tablespoons olive oil in the rinsed-out pan. Add 3 tablespoons pine nuts and cook for 1 to 2 minutes until just colored.
3 Add 2 finely chopped garlic cloves and 1 seeded and chopped red chile. Cook for 1 minute longer until the nuts are golden.
4 Stir in 3 tablespoons roughly chopped seedless raisins, together with the drained spinach, and cook for about 30 seconds or so.
5 Season well and serve.

Fennel Risotto

PREPARATION: 15 MINUTES

COOKING: 35 TO 40 MINUTES

SERVES 4 AS A MAIN COURSE OR 6 AS AN APPETIZER

2 fennel bulbs

2 tablespoons olive oil, plus more to serve

4 tablespoons butter

1 large onion, minced

1³/₄ cups risotto rice (such as Arborio)

²/₃ cup dry white wine

5 cups hot vegetable stock

¹/₂ cup freshly grated Parmesan cheese, plus more to serve

Salt and pepper

1 Core the fennel and dice; keep any fronds to garnish.

2 Heat the oil and half the butter in a large heavy-bottomed pan. Cook the onion for 5 minutes until soft and golden. Add the rice and diced fennel, and cook for 5 minutes, stirring, until the rice is slightly translucent.

3 Turn up the heat and pour in the wine; let it bubble and simmer over medium heat (this helps cook out the raw taste of the alcohol). When most of the wine has been absorbed, add a couple of ladlefuls of stock to cover the rice. Stir to prevent sticking; keep the rice on a boil. The grains will become plump and moist.

4 Cook over medium heat, stirring all the time, adding ladlefuls of stock to keep the consistency soupy. After 15 minutes, taste a grain; it should be creamy but with some bite. Don't worry if it seems a bit soupy, the rice will keep absorbing the liquid off the heat.

5 Add the remaining butter, cut in small pieces, and most of the Parmesan. Season and leave to stand for 1 minute before ladling onto plates or one large platter.

6 Scatter the risotto with a little more Parmesan, black pepper, and oil. Serve immediately, garnished with the reserved fennel fronds.

Leek and Blue Cheese Risotto

Just five ingredients can give you supper for four. Here the usual risotto procedure is simplified—all the stock is added at once, so there is no need for you to stand and stir.

PREPARATION: 15 MINUTES

COOKING: 20 TO 25 MINUTES

SERVES 4

2 large leeks

3 tablespoons olive oil

1¹/₂ cups risotto rice (such as Arborio)

3³/₄ cups hot vegetable or chicken stock

6 ounces Stilton or Danish blue cheese, crumbled

Salt and pepper

1 Trim the leeks and cut down the length to the middle. Rinse under cold water to remove any dirt. Slice thinly into rings.

2 Heat the oil in a heavy-bottomed pan that has a lid. Add the leeks and sauté quickly until bright green, about 2 minutes. Stir in the rice and cook for 2 minutes until the grains are glistening.

3 Meanwhile, in another pan, bring the stock to a boil.

4 Add the stock to the rice, stir, and bring back to a boil. Cover and simmer without stirring for 12 to 15 minutes, until the rice is tender.

5 Remove from the heat and stir in the cheese and some pepper. Taste, season if necessary, stir, and serve.

Chestnut Gnocchi with Sour Cranberries

This makes an excellent vegetarian alternative to turkey for Thanksgiving or Christmas Day.

PREPARATION: 45 MINUTES PLUS DRYING

COOKING: 45 MINUTES

SERVES 4

12 ounces baking potatoes, peeled

$1/2$ cup finely ground cooked chestnuts

$3/4$ cup grated Gruyère cheese

1 tablespoon unsalted butter

2 egg yolks

$3/4$ cup all-purpose flour

Pinch freshly grated nutmeg

FOR THE SAUCE:

1 cup vegetable stock (see page 17)

$1/3$ ounce dried wild mushrooms

4 tablespoons unsalted butter

2 shallots, minced

1 garlic clove, crushed

1 cup peeled and sliced Jerusalem artichokes

1 tablespoon balsamic vinegar

2 tablespoons tamari (Japanese soy sauce)

1 cup cranberries

1 pound small brussels sprouts, trimmed and halved

Salt and pepper

Sprigs fresh thyme, to garnish

1 Cook the potatoes in a pan of lightly salted boiling water until tender. Drain well and mash. Add the ground chestnuts and Gruyère, and beat well to let the cheese melt. Stir in the butter, egg yolks, and half the flour. Add the nutmeg and season.

2 Turn the mixture out onto a lightly floured surface and knead in the remaining flour, a little at a time, to form a smooth, soft dough; leave to cool.

3 Roll out the gnocchi dough into long rope shapes, each about 1 inch thick. Cut them into $3/4$-inch pieces. Roll each piece over the prongs of a fork to form the classic ridged and slightly curved gnocchi shape. Place the gnocchi on a lightly floured baking tray and leave to dry for 1 hour.

4 Meanwhile, make the sauce. Put the stock in a small pan and bring to a boil. Add the dried mushrooms, remove from the heat, and leave to soak for about 1 hour. Strain the mushrooms, reserving the stock.

5 Heat a skillet. Add half the butter, the shallots, garlic, artichokes, and soaked mushrooms, and cook over high heat for 5 minutes.

6 Pour in the reserved stock and cook for 10 minutes. Add the balsamic vinegar, tamari, and cranberries, and leave to simmer for 10 minutes longer.

7 Meanwhile, cook the brussels sprouts in a large pan of lightly salted boiling water for 5 to 6 minutes. Remove with a slotted spoon; reserve.

8 Poach the gnocchi, in batches, in a large pan of lightly salted boiling water, until they rise to the surface—this should take 2 to 3 minutes. Remove with a slotted spoon; drain well.

9 Melt the remaining butter in a skillet and cook the brussels sprouts and gnocchi over low heat for 2 minutes, stirring occasionally. Season with more nutmeg and salt and pepper to taste.

10 Arrange the gnocchi in a serving dish, pour the sauce over, and garnish with the sprigs of thyme.

The kneading begins in earnest. The dough will gradually lose its stickiness, so treat it as roughly as you like until you get the texture you need.

Pizza Crust

Pizzas come in two styles. The classic Neapolitan is thick and crunchy around the edge and thinner and softer in the middle. North of Rome, in big cities like Florence and Milan, they make the fashionable pizza—paper-thin, with hardly any border. Here we are making Neapolitan.

Use white bread flour here, but far nicer—and stocked by specialty food stores—is the Italian type "00," which has the best flavor.

There is no more work in making three pizzas than in making one—in our photographs a triple quantity of dough is being made. Freeze the uncooked crusts in their pans—thaw them before topping.

PREPARATION: 30 MINUTES PLUS
2½ HOURS PROVING
MAKES ONE 12-INCH PIZZA
1 cup plus 2 tablespoons water, warmed to
    105–115°F
Pinch sugar
³/₄ ounce fresh yeast, or 1 envelope quick-rise
    active-dry yeast

1 Put 3 tablespoons of the water and the sugar in a large bowl and stir in the fresh yeast. (Add the dry yeast to the flour, never to wet ingredients.) Add 4 tablespoons of the flour and mix to a soft dough (add more flour or water if necessary). Knead for 3 minutes and sprinkle with flour. Cover with a dish towel and leave to rise for 30 minutes.
2 Gently rewarm remaining water to 105–115°F. Pour remaining flour onto a work surface. Shape it into a volcano and put starter dough in crater. Pour a little water over and pinch dough, flour, and water together to mix.

After a second rise, roll out the dough to fit your pan and press it firmly in, dimpling it as you do so.

$3^1/_2$ cups Italian type "00" or all-purpose white flour, plus more if necessary

3 tablespoons extra-virgin olive oil, plus more for the baking tray

1 tablespoon salt

For the toppings, see pages 110–111

3 Gradually add some more of the water, pinching together, until all the water is added. Repeat with the olive oil. When you have added one-third of the olive oil and have a soft dough, make a dip in the top of it and then add the salt and half the remaining oil .

4 Now knead everything together until it is no longer sticky and the work surface is clean. Toss the dough and stretch it into a flat shape, drizzle with half the remaining oil, and knead. Repeat, kneading for a good minute more at the end. The dough is ready when it feels silky, but not too silky.

5 Put the dough back in the bowl and cut a cross in the top with a large, sharp knife. Sprinkle with flour, cover with a dish towel, and leave in a warm place to triple in size, about 2 hours.

6 Italians make round pizzas in pizzerias, but at home they're always rectangular—it is easier to fit in the oven! The ideal size for our recipes is a 12 × 16-inch baking sheet with a shallow rim. Grease it with extra-virgin olive oil. Lightly flour your work surface and scoop the dough out onto it. Knead it or roll it for a few minutes, then press it evenly into the pan, leaving it heavily indented with your fingertips—it should be slightly thinner in the middle. Prick it all over with a fork. See pages 110–111 for topping ideas and baking directions.

Pizza Toppings

Prepare your toppings as follows.
Preheat the oven to 475°F. Add the
topping and bake for 18 to 20 minutes
until the pizza is puffed and golden.
Don't open the oven for the first 15
minutes or you'll let the heat out and
your crust won't be as crisp.

PIZZA CON MENTA ZUCCHINE
MINT AND ZUCCHINI PIZZA

Slice 3 zucchini at an angle and quarter
a garlic clove. Stir-fry in 3 tablespoons
extra-virgin olive oil for 6 to 8 minutes.
Leave to cool, then remove the garlic.
Mix with 1 heaping cup chopped fresh
mozzarella (preferably buffalo), a
handful of chopped mint, and salt and
pepper. Spread over the dough, sprinkle
with extra-virgin olive oil and salt and
black pepper.

PIZZA NAPOLETANA

Drain 2 (14 ounce) cans plum tomatoes
and chop. Seed and chop a red chile
(optional). Sprinkle over pizza and top
with extra-virgin olive oil, oregano, and
salt and pepper. Drain a (2 ounce) can
of anchovy fillets and crumble them over
the top. Sprinkle with more oregano and
olive oil.

PIZZA BIANCA CON SEMI DE
FINOCCHIO E FORMAGGIO
FENNEL SEED AND CHEESE PIZZA

Mix 4 heaped tablespoons each full-fat
cream cheese, ricotta, and crème fraîche.
Season with black pepper and spread over
the dough. Drizzle extra-virgin olive oil
over and sprinkle with 3 tablespoons
fennel seeds and more pepper.

PIZZA AL FUNGHI E RICOTTA
MUSHROOM AND RICOTTA PIZZA
Break up ¹/₃ ounce dried porcini and
soak in warm water for 15 minutes;
drain. Drain 2 (14 ounce) cans plum
tomatoes and chop roughly. Mix in a
bowl with a little salt, 2 tablespoons
extra-virgin olive oil, and a few roughly
torn basil leaves. Slice 8 ounces mixed
mushrooms (crimini, chanterelle, oyster,
or other) and sauté in 2 tablespoons
extra-virgin olive oil with the dried
mushrooms and a quartered garlic clove
for 6 to 8 minutes, until brown and
nutty-smelling; remove the garlic.
Spread the tomato mixture over the
dough, spoon the mushrooms over, and
dot 1 cup ricotta and some more
shredded basil over the top.

PIZZA CON PORRI E PEPE NERO
LEEK AND BLACK PEPPER PIZZA
Sauté 3 thinly sliced leeks in 3
tablespoons extra-virgin olive oil and
season. Spread dough with 1 cup crème
fraîche or sour cream, top with the leeks,
Parmesan shavings, black pepper, and
more oil.

PIZZA CON RUCOLA
ARUGULA PIZZA
Prick the dough all over with a fork,
brush with 4 tablespoons extra-virgin
olive oil, and sprinkle with sea salt. Bake
for 15 to 18 minutes until golden. Cover
with 1¹/₄ pounds cherry tomato quarters,
a handful of torn arugula leaves, and
1¹/₄ cups chopped fresh mozzarella
cheese (preferably buffalo). Drizzle with
olive oil.

Tomato and Oregano Pizza

This is a version of the classic Pizza Napoletana without the anchovies.

PREPARATION: 5 MINUTES
BAKING: 15 TO 20 MINUTES
MAKES ONE 12-INCH PIZZA (SERVES 2 TO 4)

1 beefsteak tomato, sliced
1 prepared Pizza Crust (see pages 108–9)
1 quantity Old-Fashioned Tomato Sauce (see page 20)
8 yellow cherry tomatoes, halved
8 red cherry tomatoes, halved
1 garlic clove, thinly sliced
1 tablespoon extra-virgin olive oil
Salt and pepper
2 teaspoons fresh oregano leaves

1 Preheat the oven to 425°F. Layer the beefsteak tomato slices over the pizza crust. Spread the tomato sauce over them. Scatter the cherry tomatoes and garlic over. Drizzle with the oil and season with salt and black pepper.
2 Bake for 15 to 20 minutes, until the pizza is golden at the edge and the tomatoes are lightly charred.
3 Scatter the oregano over, just before serving.

Pimiento, Arugula, and Mozzarella Pizza

The mozzarella cheese originally used for pizzas was traditionally made from the milk of water buffaloes. Today cows milk is more commonly used, although the results are often more bland and rubbery than the authentic mozzarella di bufala. *You can't do better than homemade pesto, but for speed use sauce from a jar instead. Taste it first, because some brands can be too salty.*

PREPARATION: 15 MINUTES
BAKING: 15 TO 20 MINUTES
MAKES ONE 12-INCH PIZZA (SERVES 2 TO 4)

$1/4$ cup fresh basil leaves
1 tablespoon grated Parmesan cheese
1 garlic clove, halved
2 teaspoons pine nuts
3 tablespoons olive oil
1 prepared Pizza Crust (see pages 108–9)
1 (14 ounce) can pimientos, drained and sliced
5 ounces fresh mozzarella cheese, sliced
1 ounce arugula leaves

1 Preheat the oven to 425°F. Place the basil, Parmesan, garlic, and pine nuts in a food processor and process until coarsely chopped. With the motor still running, gradually add the oil to make a smooth paste.
2 Spread the pesto over the pizza crust and arrange the sliced pimientos and mozzarella on top.
3 Bake for 15 to 20 minutes, until puffed and golden.
4 Scatter the arugula over and leave to wilt slightly before serving.

We take potatoes so much for granted we almost stop thinking of them as vegetables—and treat them like mere fillers. The humble potato is, however, as versatile as any leaf or stem, and can feature in dishes as diverse as delicate potato cakes for sophisticated appetizers, comforting flavored purees, and that culinary miracle—the glorious French fry.

Staple Diet

Ways with Potatoes

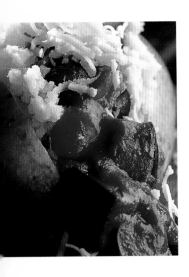

Ways with Baked Potatoes

The best baking potatoes are large and starchy, such as Idaho or russet.

BASIC BAKED POTATO

SERVES 4

Preheat the oven to 400°F. Prick skins of 4 large, scrubbed, and dried baking potatoes. Bake 1 to 1½ hours. Wearing an oven glove, squeeze gently—they should feel soft. Cut a cross in top, and fluff the flesh with a fork. Add 1 tablespoon butter to each and season.

VARIATION: Microwaving is faster, but finishing in the oven gives the skin the right texture. Prepare the potatoes as above; rub with olive oil and salt. Cook following microwave directions, then bake for 15 to 20 minutes in a 400°F oven.

BLUE CHEESE AND HERB POTATOES

SERVES 4

Bake 4 potatoes as above and cool slightly (leave oven on). Melt 2 tablespoons butter in a pan and sauté 1 crushed garlic clove and 2 chopped scallions for 2 minutes. Remove the potato flesh, leaving the skin intact, and mash. Fold in the garlic mixture with 4 tablespoons sour cream, 4 ounces crumbled blue cheese, 1 tablespoon each chopped fresh parsley and chives. Season and spoon into the skins, mounding. Bake for 10 to 15 minutes.

SPINACH, MUSHROOM AND EGG POTATOES

SERVES 2

Heat 1 tablespoon olive oil in a pan. Add 1 small finely chopped onion and 2 crushed garlic cloves, and sauté 3 to 5 minutes. Add 2½ cups sliced mushrooms and cook until golden. Season. Add 4 cups shredded spinach and simmer 3 to 4 minutes until liquid evaporates. Add 3 tablespoons mascarpone and cook 2 minutes. Cut a cross in top of each potato and squeeze open. Fluff the flesh with a fork. Spoon in the mixture, making a hollow. Crack an egg into each, season, and cover with foil. Bake 10 to 15 minutes until whites set. Sprinkle with grated Parmesan.

EGGPLANT-CHILE POTATOES

SERVES 4

Heat 2 tablespoons oil. Add 1 sliced red onion and sauté 4 to 5 minutes. Add 1½ cups diced eggplant and 1 diced red bell pepper, and cook 5 to 8 minutes. Stir in 1 small finely chopped red chile, 2 finely chopped garlic cloves, and 1 teaspoon ground cumin. Add 1 (14 ounce) can crushed tomatoes, 1 teaspoon tomato paste, 1 drained (14 ounce) can kidney beans, and 1¼ cups water. Simmer 15 to 20 minutes until vegetables are soft. Season. Fluff the flesh of 4 hot baked potatoes. Spoon the chile over and top with 1 cup grated smoked cheddar.

HUMMUS AND AVOCADO SALSA POTATOES

SERVES 4

Dice ¼ cucumber, 2 plum tomatoes, 1 red onion, and 1 peeled avocado; mix well. Whisk together the juice of 1 lemon, 2 tablespoons extra-virgin olive oil, and 3 tablespoons chopped cilantro. Season and pour over the salsa. Split 4 potatoes baked as above and fluff the flesh. Spoon in 1⅓ cups hummus and top with salsa.

Oven Egg and Fries

PREPARATION: 10 MINUTES
BAKING: 40 TO 45 MINUTES
SERVES 2

1 pound baking potatoes, such as Idahos

2 garlic cloves, peeled and sliced

4 rosemary sprigs, or 1 teaspoon dried

2 tablespoons olive oil

Salt and pepper

2 eggs

1 Preheat the oven to 425°F. Cut the potatoes into thick French fries.

2 Add the French fries to a roasting pan (a nonstick pan is best). Sprinkle the sliced garlic over. Strip the rosemary needles from the sprigs and sprinkle the needles over. Drizzle with the olive oil and season. Toss to coat the French fries in the oil and all the flavorings.

3 Bake for 35 to 40 minutes until the French fries are just cooked and golden in color, shaking the pan about halfway through.

4 Make 2 gaps in the fries and break an egg into each gap. Return to the oven for 3 to 5 minutes until the eggs are cooked to your liking.

VARIATIONS: If you can get hold of some, a little goose fat used instead of the oil will give you the most delicious results. Instead of the rosemary, you can flavor the fries with some dried thyme or a little chile or curry powder.

Spiced Roasted Potatoes

Sweet potatoes are delicious roasted, but they cook more quickly than regular potatoes, so you will need to parboil the baking potatoes for a few minutes, to soften them, before roasting them with the sweet ones.

PREPARATION: 15 MINUTES
ROASTING: 40 TO 50 MINUTES
SERVES 4

1 pound baking potatoes, unpeeled

1 pound sweet potatoes, peeled

4 tablespoons olive oil

2 tablespoons butter

1 teaspoon ground turmeric

1 teaspoon chile powder

1 teaspoon curry powder

1 teaspoon light brown sugar

Salt and pepper

2 tablespoons chopped fresh cilantro

1 Preheat the oven to 400°F. Place the baking potatoes in a pan, cover with cold water, and bring to a boil. Simmer for 10 minutes; drain and pat dry. Leave to cool slightly, then peel. Cut the baking potatoes and sweet potatoes into equal-size cubes.

2 Place the oil and butter in a roasting pan and heat until the butter melts and is foaming. Add the spices and sugar, and stir. Add the potatoes to the pan, coating them all over in the oil and spices.

3 Roast for 40 to 50 minutes until tender. Season well and sprinkle with the cilantro.

Steps to making Garlic and Rosemary Roasties (opposite), with and without the red onions.

Roasted Potatoes

To guarantee crisp potatoes, make sure they are completely dry before they go into the oven. Resist the urge to turn the potatoes too often; let them brown on one side before turning. Do not salt the potatoes until the end of cooking—salting beforehand encourages them to give up their liquid, making them limp.

PREPARATION: 30 TO 35 MINUTES

ROASTING: 45 TO 50 MINUTES

SERVES 4

2 pounds baking potatoes, such as
   russets, unpeeled

Salt and pepper

3 tablespoons olive oil

1 Preheat the oven to 400°F. Place the potatoes in a pan, cover with cold water, add a little salt, bring to a boil, and cook for 10 to 15 minutes until tender, gently shaking the pan halfway through; drain well. Let cool slightly and peel. Cut the potatoes into even-size pieces.

2 Heat the oil in a roasting pan in the oven until very hot, about 10 minutes. Add the potatoes and turn them so they are evenly coated with oil.

3 Roast for 30 minutes. Remove from oven, turn, and roast for 15 to 20 minutes longer, or until brown and crunchy on the outside. Season well.

Red Onion, Garlic, and Rosemary Roasties

These mouthwatering potatoes are a fine accompaniment to anything from roasted meat to a cheese soufflé. The key is to use small, firm potatoes—the smaller they are cut, the quicker they will cook.

PREPARATION: 10 MINUTES
ROASTING: 30 TO 35 MINUTES
SERVES 4

$1^1/_2$–$1^3/_4$ pounds small, firm new potatoes

2 tablespoons butter

2 tablespoons olive oil

2 red onions, cut into chunks

8 garlic cloves, unpeeled

2 tablespoons chopped fresh rosemary

Salt and pepper

1 Preheat the oven to 450°F. Peel the potatoes and cut into quarters. Rinse well and pat dry thoroughly.

2 Place the butter and oil in a roasting pan and heat in the oven until the butter melts and is foaming. Add the potatoes, red onions, garlic, and rosemary, and toss well, making sure the potatoes and onions are sitting in a single layer.

3 Place the pan in the oven and roast for about 25 minutes, shaking the pan occasionally to turn the potatoes, until golden and tender when tested with a fork.

4 When the potatoes are cooked, season to taste with sea salt and freshly ground black pepper.

Hasselback Potatoes

Hasselback Potatoes are named for the Stockholm restaurant of the same name. Versions of this dish are also known by various descriptive terms, like "hedgehog potatoes" or even "toast-rack" potatoes.

PREPARATION: 30 MINUTES
ROASTING: 40 TO 50 MINUTES
SERVES 4

2 pounds potatoes
Coarse sea salt
1 tablespoon sunflower oil
4 tablespoons butter
1 teaspoon paprika

1 Preheat the oven to 400°F. Peel the potatoes and place them in a pan of cold water with a little salt. Bring to a boil. Lower the heat and simmer for 10 to 15 minutes; drain well and pat dry.
2 Beginning 1/2 inch in from the end, carefully make cuts 1/8 inch apart along the potato, but without cutting all the way through.
3 Heat the oil and butter in a small pan and add the paprika.
4 Place the potatoes in a roasting pan and brush them with the flavored oil and butter. Roast for 40 to 50 minutes until golden brown and tender.
5 Serve sprinkled with the sea salt.

VARIATIONS: Roast the potatoes on a bed of peeled garlic cloves for even more flavor. Or replace the paprika with chile powder or dried rosemary. You can also consider stuffing the cuts in the potatoes with tapenade, chopped anchovies, or slices of a melting cheese, such as Brie or mozzarella.

Scalloped Potato and Rich Cheese Tart

The cheese provides a tangy counterpoint to the rich cream and mild potatoes, making this a luxurious dish.

PREPARATION: 15 MINUTES
COOKING: 55 MINUTES
SERVES 4 AS AN APPETIZER, OR 6 AS A SIDE DISH

2 cups milk
2/3 cup heavy cream
1 garlic clove
3 pounds potatoes, sliced into thin rounds
Pinch freshly grated nutmeg
8 ounces Vacherin, Camembert, or Reblochon cheese
2 tablespoons butter, softened
Salt and pepper

1 In a large, deep flameproof casserole or skillet, bring the milk and cream to a gentle simmer with the garlic. Add the potatoes in 2 batches to poach slowly, uncovered, for 5 minutes until almost cooked but not falling apart. Lift out the slices with a slotted spoon and transfer to a plate. Remove the garlic when soft (with the first batch) and reserve.
2 Preheat the oven to 400°F. Drain any excess milk from the potatoes back into the pan and add nutmeg.
3 Wipe the cheese with paper towels, pare away any hard bits of rind, and cut the cheese into slices. Add one-third of the slices to the milk and heat until melted; there will be bits of the rind, but it is fine to leave them in.
4 Crush the softened garlic clove and mash into the butter, and use to grease a 9 × 13 inch gratin or baking dish. Lay one-third of the potato slices overlapping in the bottom of the dish. Lay half the remaining cheese slices on top. Pour one-third of the cheesy milk mixture over and season. Continue layering in the same way; don't fill dish more than two-thirds full, as it will bubble up. Pour the remaining milk mixture over the final potato layer. Season lightly.
5 Bake for about 50 minutes until golden brown and cooked through.

There are hundreds of different potato varieties, and each country has developed its own to suit tastes and growing conditions. Stores now sell far more types, making it possible to experiment.

For the American cook, however, potatoes fall into four basic categories: Long whites, round whites, round reds, and russets. Long whites are all-purpose potatoes with thin skins and a waxy texture. Round whites, also thin skinned, are best for frying and boiling. Round reds, with a firm, waxy texture, are best suited to boiling. Russets are favored for baking and frying because of their dry, fluffy texture. The popular Idaho potato is an example of a russet.

When you are shopping, look for potatoes with clean, smooth skins and a firm texture. Do not buy any with green spots or mold.

Potatoes

Potatoes Sautéed with Garlic and Onion

PREPARATION: 15 MINUTES
COOKING: 35 MINUTES
SERVES 4

1 Cook 2 pounds waxy potatoes, unpeeled, in boiling salted water for 10 minutes until almost soft. Drain, peel, and, if large, cut into even-size dice.

2 Heat 2 tablespoons olive oil and 4 tablespoons butter in a heavy-bottomed skillet. Add the potatoes and fry for 10 minutes until beginning to brown.

3 Add 1 thinly sliced onion and 3 finely chopped garlic cloves. Cook for 5 minutes longer until crisp and golden.

4 Serve sprinkled with 2 tablespoons chopped parsley and some salt and pepper.

Pan Haggerty

Slice the potatoes for this layered cake on a mandoline or use the slicing attachment on a food processor. This way the slices will be an even thickness so that they all cook in the same time.

PREPARATION: 15 MINUTES
COOKING: 50 MINUTES
SERVES 4

1 pound firm potatoes
3 tablespoons sunflower oil
1 onion, thinly sliced
1 cup grated cheddar cheese
Salt and pepper

1 Peel the potatoes and cut them into very thin slices (see above). Rinse the slices well and pat them dry on paper towels.
2 Heat the oil slowly in a nonstick skillet. Make layers of potatoes, onion, and cheese, seasoning between each layer and finishing with a layer of potatoes. Cook over low heat for 30 minutes until the bottom is browned, then turn over (as for the Rösti, see page 128) and brown for 20 minutes longer.
3 Serve cut into wedges.

VARIATIONS: Add a layer of sliced tomato between the onion and the cheese for a moister dish. Replace half the potatoes with slices of celery root for a delicious accompaniment to game dishes. Gruyère cheese also produces good results, so you can use it instead of the cheddar.

Stoved New Potatoes and Mushrooms

This way of cooking new potatoes is adapted from an old Scottish recipe, traditionally using meat stock. Here, the savoriness comes instead from olives and dried mushrooms and their soaking liquid. The potatoes are eaten smeared with the garlic, which cooks to a deliciously mild finish.

PREPARATION: 10 MINUTES
COOKING: 25 MINUTES
SERVES 2

1 tablespoon crumbled dried porcini mushrooms
1¼ cups hot vegetable stock
1 tablespoon olive oil
4 plump garlic cloves, unpeeled
8 ripe olives
2 small sprigs of fresh rosemary, plus extra to serve
1–1¼ pounds new potatoes, cut into ¼ inch slices
1½ cups sliced crimini mushrooms
Salt and pepper
Chopped fresh flat-leaf parsley, to serve (optional)

1 Place the mushrooms in a measuring cup and pour the hot stock over; leave to soak while you prepare the vegetables.
2 Heat the oil in a heavy skillet with a lid. Add the whole garlic cloves, olives, and rosemary, and cook for 2 minutes.
3 Add half the potatoes, to cover the bottom of the pan. Remove the porcini mushrooms from the liquid with a slotted spoon and scatter, with the crimini mushrooms, over the potatoes. Cover with the remaining potatoes. Pour the reserved mushroom liquid over and add plenty of seasoning.
4 Cover and cook for 15 minutes. Remove the lid and cook for 5 minutes longer, until the potatoes are tender and almost all the liquid has been absorbed.
5 Divide between 2 warmed serving plates. Discard the rosemary, adding fresh leaves with the parsley, if desired.
6 To eat, cut off the end of each of the garlic cloves and press out the creamy flesh to eat with the potatoes.

Potato Rösti

Traditionally made as one large flat cake, rösti can also be made in individual servings.

PREPARATION: 10 MINUTES
COOKING: 30 MINUTES
SERVES 4

2 pounds potatoes, unpeeled

Salt and pepper

2 tablespoons butter

1 tablespoon olive oil

1 Cook the potatoes in boiling lightly salted water for 10 minutes until almost soft. Remove from the pan and leave to cool in their skins. Peel and grate the flesh coarsely; season.

2 In a 9 inch nonstick skillet, heat the butter and oil until very hot. Spread the potato evenly in the pan, reduce the heat, and cook for 10 minutes.

3 Turn the rösti over by placing a plate or board over the pan and inverting it onto the plate. Slide the rösti back into the pan, cooked-side up, and continue to cook for 10 minutes longer, until cooked underneath.

4 Serve cut into wedges.

Potato Latkes with Herb-Broiled Feta

Latke is the Jewish name for a pancake made with grated potatoes, similar to rösti.

PREPARATION: 25 MINUTES
COOKING: 55 MINUTES
SERVES 4

1 large potato, peeled and coarsely grated

1 onion, coarsely grated

1 egg, beaten

2 tablespoons all-purpose flour

2 tablespoons vegetable oil

2 teaspoons small capers, drained, to serve

FOR THE CHILE JAM:

2¹/₂ tablespoons butter

2 onions, thinly sliced

¹/₄ cup sugar

6 tablespoons red-wine vinegar

1 red chile, seeded and finely chopped

FOR THE HERB-BROILED FETA:

6 tablespoons olive oil

1 garlic clove, crushed

1 teaspoon each chopped fresh oregano and thyme

Salt and pepper

9 ounces feta cheese

1 To make the chile jam, first melt the butter in a pan. Then add the onions and cook for 6 to 8 minutes until golden and soft. Add the sugar and red-wine vinegar, and cook slowly for 25 minutes longer. Add the chile and cook for 5 to 10 minutes longer, until the onions are caramelized and bright red; keep the mixture hot.

2 Meanwhile, make the latkes. Take the grated potato in your hands and squeeze together to extract as much moisture and starch as possible. Pat dry on paper towels and place in a bowl. Add the onion, beaten egg, and flour, and mix well.

3 Heat half the oil in a large, nonstick skillet. Divide the potato mixture into 4 and add 2 of these portions to the pan. Flatten slightly and fry for 3 to 4 minutes on each side until crisp and golden; keep warm. Heat the remaining oil and cook the other 2 portions; keep warm.

4 Make the herb-broiled feta: Preheat the broiler and mix together the olive oil, garlic, oregano, thyme, and seasoning. Cut the feta into 4 equal slices. Arrange these in the broiler pan and coat with half the olive oil mixture. Broil for 2 to 3 minutes until slightly melted.

5 To serve, place the latkes on serving plates and top with a spoonful of the chile jam. Place the broiled feta on top and sprinkle a few capers over; drizzle with a little of the remaining olive oil mixture.

Soufflé Potatoes

These are thin slices of potato cooked in exactly the same way as French fries until they are puffed up and golden.

When choosing oil for deep-frying, you need to use one that has a relatively high smoke-point, meaning that it can be heated to a high temperature before starting to break down. It should also be relatively flavorless, so its flavor will not overpower that of the potato or other food being fried. Sunflower, peanut, or a pure vegetable oil is ideal.

PREPARATION: 15 MINUTES

COOKING: 10 TO 15 MINUTES

SERVES 4

3 baking potatoes

Peanut oil for deep-frying

Salt

1 Peel the potatoes and cut them into ¼-inch slices (slightly thicker than that required for potato chips). Wipe them dry—do not put them in water!

2 Heat the oil to 375°F and fry the potato slices in batches for 1 to 2 minutes. Drain on paper towels. Repeat with the remaining potatoes.

3 Heat the oil again until it reaches 400°F. Add the potatoes to the oil, again in batches. They will puff up and brown; drain each batch well.

4 Serve the soufflé potatoes sprinkled with salt.

VARIATION: For an attractive multicolored special-occasion accompaniment, make these with a mixture of sliced roots, including celery root, parsnips, and beets.

French Fries

The size of the French fry determines how much fat is absorbed. Thinly cut fries have a greater surface area compared to their middles and are therefore a lot higher in fat than fat wedges.

PREPARATION: 15 MINUTES
COOKING: 10 TO 15 MINUTES
SERVES 4
Peanut oil for deep-frying
4 large baking potatoes
Salt

1 Preheat the oven to 325°F. Half fill a heavy-bottomed, medium-size pan or deep-fat fryer with the oil.

2 Peel the potatoes, rinse, and cut in strips about ¹/₂ inch wide and 2 inches long; place in a bowl of cold water as they are prepared.

3 Thoroughly dry a batch of cut potatoes on paper towels. To test that the oil is ready, drop in a cube of bread; if it sizzles and turns brown in 5 to 10 seconds, the oil is hot enough. Alternatively, if you have a frying thermometer, the temperature of the oil at this stage should be 375°F. Place the potatoes in a frying basket and lower into the oil. Fry for 5 to 6 minutes, shaking the basket a few times to guarantee even cooking. Lift out and drain the fries on paper towels; continue to cook the remaining potatoes.

4 Heat the oil to 400°F and fry the part-cooked potatoes, in batches, in the hot oil for 2 to 3 minutes until golden brown. Drain thoroughly on paper towels and place on a hot serving plate. Keep hot in the oven (with the door slightly open or the fries will lose their crispness) while you continue frying the remaining French fries.

5 When all the fries are ready, serve them sprinkled with salt.

Mash and More

For the best mashed potatoes, cook the potatoes whole and unpeeled to prevent them from becoming waterlogged.

BASIC MASHED POTATOES

SERVES 4

Cook 2 pounds unpeeled potatoes in boiling salted water; drain. When cool enough to handle, peel and return to pan with 4 tablespoons butter. Mash over low heat until smooth. Gradually add ⅔ cup hot milk and beat until creamy; season.

ALIGOT

SERVES 4

Make the mashed potatoes as above, adding 4 tablespoons heavy cream with the butter. Mash over low heat. Instead of milk, beat in 1 crushed garlic clove, then add 1¼ cups grated Gruyère cheese, a little at a time. The potatoes are ready when they are shiny and come away from sides of the pan; season well.

LEEK AND MUSTARD MASHED POTATOES

SERVES 4

Heat 2 tablespoons olive oil in a pan. Fry 2 large finely chopped leeks for 7 to 10 minutes. Mix the leeks into Basic Mashed Potatoes as above with 2 tablespoons grain mustard and 1 cup grated Cheddar.

HERB AND PARMESAN MASHED POTATOES

SERVES 4

Mix ½ cup grated Parmesan into the Basic Mashed Potatoes as above. Then beat in an additional tablespoon of butter, together with 3 tablespoons each chopped parsley and basil. Season.

CHAMP

SERVES 4

For this classic Irish dish, chop a bunch of scallions, including the green tops, and put in a pan with 1¼ cups milk. Bring to a boil, lower the heat, and simmer for 2 to 3 minutes. Remove from the heat and leave to infuse for about 10 minutes.

Use the milk mixture to make the Basic Mashed Potatoes as above, instead of the plain, hot milk; reheat, if necessary, in a clean pan. Spoon into small serving bowls. Make a hollow in the top of each and add some more butter and some crumbled blue cheese, if you like. Dip forkfuls of the mashed potatoes in the melted butter (and cheese) to eat.

COLCANNON

SERVES 4

To make this other traditional Irish dish, replace the scallions in the Champ with shredded cabbage or kale and omit the blue cheese. Serve it like the Champ, with melted butter, or fry it in the butter in small, flat cakes.

CLAPSHOT

SERVES 4

This Scottish dish is made like Champ but without cheese and using equal quantities potatoes and rutabagas ("neeps" in Scotland). You can also beat in chopped chives or bacon fat for extra flavor, if you like. The added chopped scallions are optional.

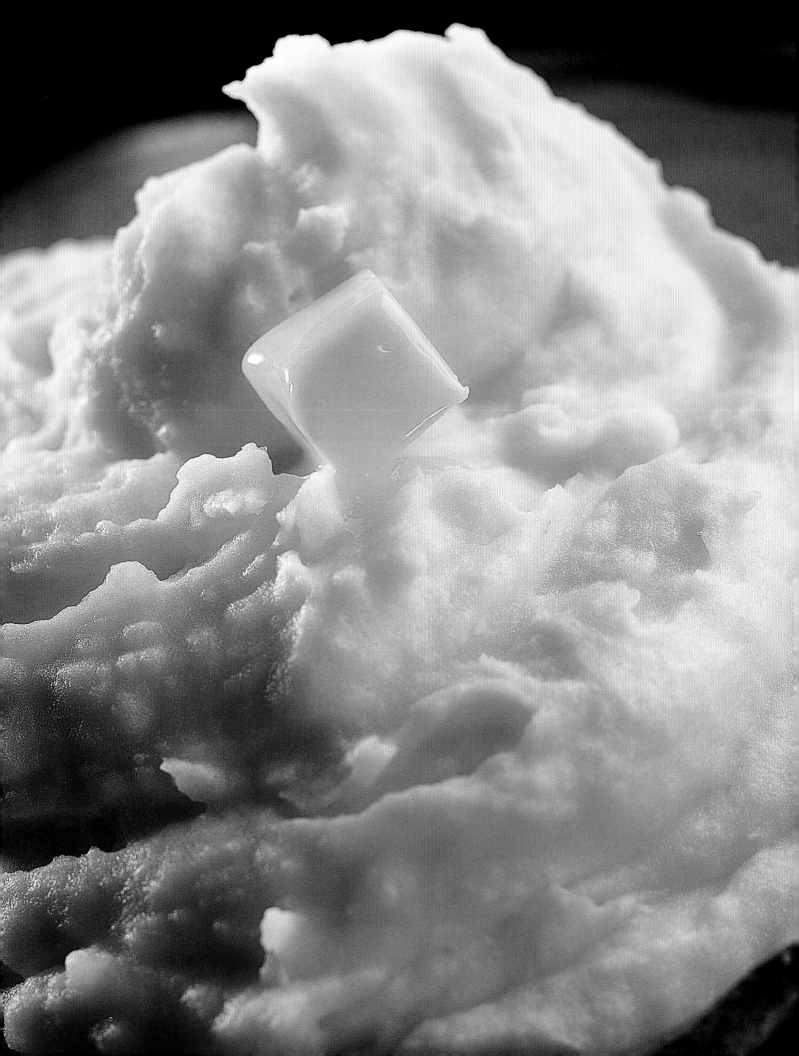

Perhaps no style of cooking makes better use of vegetable crunch, color, and vigor than the cuisines of Asia, where it is traditional to cook vegetables quickly to preserve their best properties. Enjoy steaming stir-fries, flavor-packed noodle dishes, and piquant salads, as well as subtly spiced curries and crisp mouthwatering fillings for egg rolls.

Stirring it up

Asian Ways with Vegetables

Spring Vegetable Noodles

PREPARATION: 15 MINUTES

COOKING: 10 TO 15 MINUTES

SERVES 4

2 tablespoons olive oil

1 tablespoon chopped fresh parsley

1 egg, beaten

8 ounces medium egg noodles

2 garlic cloves, minced

2 inch piece ginger root, cut into sticks

2 carrots, cut into sticks

4 ounces portobello mushrooms, thickly sliced

4 ounces sugar snap peas

8 ounces leeks, sliced into strips

2 tablespoons soy sauce

2/3 cup vegetable stock

1 Heat half the oil in a large skillet. Mix the parsley and egg and pour into the skillet to make a thin omelet. Cook for 1 minute until set, flip, and cook for 30 seconds more. Put on a plate.

2 Cook the noodles according to the package directions.

3 Meanwhile, heat the remaining oil in the skillet, toss in the garlic and ginger, and stir-fry over moderate heat for about 30 seconds. Add the carrots and mushrooms, and cook over high heat for a few minutes, stirring occasionally. Add the sugar snap peas and the leeks and stir-fry for 2 minutes. Season. Pour in the soy sauce and stock, and cook over high heat for about 1 minute.

4 Cut the omelet in thin strips. When the noodles are ready, drain, and spoon onto serving plates. Top with the vegetables in their juices and pile the omelet strips on top.

Udon Noodles with Miso and Roasted Ginger Pumpkin

You can use frozen or dried udon noodles, both available from Asian grocery stores. You will also find vacuum-packed noodles in supermarkets.

PREPARATION: 25 MINUTES

COOKING: 45 MINUTES

SERVES 4

FOR THE ROASTED GINGER PUMPKIN:

$1^3/_4$ pounds pumpkin or winter squash, peeled, seeded, and cut into bite-size pieces

3 tablespoons vegetable oil

2 tablespoons grated fresh ginger root

Sea salt flakes

$2^1/_2$ cups vegetable stock

1 tablespoon dark miso paste

$^1/_4$ cup soy sauce

8 ounces Japanese udon noodles

1 head of bok choy, leaves separated

1 leek, trimmed, halved, and shredded

$1^1/_4$-inch piece fresh ginger root, peeled and finely shredded

4 scallions, trimmed and sliced

1 tablespoon fresh cilantro leaves, to garnish

2 teaspoons toasted sesame oil (optional)

1 To prepare the pumpkin, preheat the oven to 400°F. Place the pumpkin in a large roasting pan and toss with the oil, ginger, and sea salt. Roast for 40 minutes, until golden and soft.

2 Mix together the stock, miso paste, and soy sauce in a pan. Stir in the noodles, bok choy, leek, pumpkin, ginger, and scallions, and cook for 3 minutes, until the noodles are heated through.

3 Divide the noodle mixture and broth among 4 warm serving bowls. Scatter the cilantro on top and drizzle sesame oil over, if desired, before serving.

Hoisin Chinese Noodles

A package of noodles and a few dried shiitake mushrooms help make a flavorful meal from various fresh or canned vegetables. Most Asian-style noodles are suitable for this dish, but check the directions, because some might need precooking rather than just soaking.

PREPARATION: 20 MINUTES
COOKING: 10 MINUTES
SERVES 4

2 ounces dry shiitake mushrooms

8 ounces medium Chinese egg noodles

3 tablespoons sesame oil

2 garlic cloves, crushed

$^1/_2$ teaspoon finely chopped fresh ginger root

Bunch scallions, roughly chopped

5 ounces sugar snap peas

4 ounces asparagus tips

2 cups diced tofu

$^2/_3$ cup bottled hoisin sauce (Chinese barbecue sauce)

2 tablespoons soy sauce

Salt and pepper

Fresh cilantro leaves, to garnish

1 Rinse the mushrooms; soak them in tepid water for 30 minutes. Drain, reserving the liquid, and roughly chop. Soak the noodles according to the package directions; drain thoroughly.
2 Heat the oil in a large nonstick wok or skillet over high heat. Add the garlic, ginger, and mushrooms, and as soon as they sizzle, toss in the remaining vegetables and stir-fry for 3 minutes.
3 Add the diced tofu, 2 tablespoons of the reserved mushroom soaking liquid, the hoisin sauce, and the soy sauce. Stir-fry until the sauce boils. Add the drained noodles and toss together over the heat until piping hot. Season to taste.
4 Serve garnished with fresh cilantro leaves.

VARIATIONS: Replace the tofu with $^1/_2$ cup roasted cashew nuts, or add protein in the form of a 3-egg omelet, rolled and sliced, scattered over the finished stir-fry.

You can use green beans, baby corn, sliced bell peppers, or bean sprouts instead of sugar snap peas and asparagus.

Vegetable Stir-Fry with Phyllo "Noodles"

The texture of firm tofu is improved by brisk stir-frying. Crunchy phyllo pastry "noodles" make a healthy alternative to fried noodles.

PREPARATION: 15 MINUTES
COOKING: ABOUT 15 MINUTES
SERVES 2

5 ounces firm tofu cubes

4 sheets phyllo pastry dough

1 tablespoon oil

$^1/_2$ teaspoon cornstarch

6 large scallions, thickly sliced

1 red bell pepper, seeded and sliced

Heaping 1 cup broccoli cut into small florets

$1^1/_4$ cups fresh bean sprouts

FOR THE MARINADE:

1 garlic clove, crushed

$^3/_4$-inch piece fresh ginger root, chopped

1 tablespoon soy sauce

3 tablespoons dry sherry or rice wine

2 teaspoons bottled sweet chile sauce

1 Preheat the oven to 375°F. To make the marinade, mix the ingredients together in a shallow glass dish. Toss the tofu in the soy mixture to coat. Leave to marinate while you prepare the remaining ingredients.

2 Roll up the phyllo dough sheets and slice into $^1/_2$-inch-wide ribbons. Use your fingers to separate them and spread out evenly on a cookie sheet. Bake for 8 minutes until crisp and pale golden.

3 Meanwhile, heat the oil in a wok or large pan. Lift the tofu out of the marinade with a slotted spoon and stir-fry for 2 minutes; reserve the marinade.

4 Mix the cornstarch with 2 tablespoons water and stir into the marinade. Remove the tofu from the wok and return to the marinade.

5 Add the scallions, pepper, and broccoli to the wok, and stir-fry for 2 minutes. Add the bean sprouts and the tofu mixture. Stir-fry until the marinade comes to a boil and thickens.

6 Divide the phyllo noodles between 2 plates and spoon the stir-fry on top. Serve immediately.

Lime-yellow, flame-orange, fire-engine red and nightshade purple—and every shade in between; there are 3,000-odd varieties of chile, and they open up a whole new world of flavor. Chiles originated in South America, but their unique properties quickly won them a pivotal role in the cooking of most continents. Size, shape, and color are little guide to either heat or flavor; although, in general, the smaller they are, the hotter they tend to be. The habanero or Scotch bonnet is probably the hottest known, thin red and green Thai chiles have fairly good heat and an intriguing taste, while the torpedo-shaped jalapeño is medium-hot and has lots of fruity flavor.

Look for firm glossy specimens, with no trace of mold or looseness about the stems. Store them in loose plastic bags in the salad drawer of the refrigerator. The heat of the chile lies in the capsaicin, the oily substance found in the seeds and the pale membrane that connects them to the flesh; so some or all of these should be removed if you don't want too fierce a result. Always wash your hands carefully after you have handled chiles as the capsaicin can burn sensitive areas like the eyes.

Chiles

Chile Oil

Use this easy-to-make chile oil as a flavoring—add a drop to salad dressings or cooked pasta, brush it over broiled fish, or stir a little into tomato-based sauces. You could also float a fresh chile in the oil and serve it as a condiment.

1 Gently heat $2^1/_2$ cups vegetable or corn oil in a saucepan.
2 Halve 4 fresh, medium-hot red chiles, lengthwise and cook gently for 5 minutes. You can leave the seeds in or remove some or all of them, depending on how hot you want the chile oil to be. Set aside overnight for the flavor and color to develop.
3 The next day, strain the oil into sterilized bottles and seal. Store for up to 6 months.

Brussels Sprouts with Peanut Sauce

PREPARATION: 10 MINUTES

COOKING: ABOUT 10 MINUTES

SERVES 4

18 ounces brussels sprouts

1 tablespoon smooth peanut butter

5 tablespoons soy sauce

2 tablespoons sunflower oil

4 tablespoons toasted pine nuts, roughly
    chopped

1 In a pan of boiling water, cook the brussels sprouts for 5 to 6 minutes until just tender; drain well.

2 In a small bowl, mix the peanut butter with 4 tablespoons of the soy sauce and stir until a smooth paste forms.

3 Heat the oil in a wok or large skillet. Quickly stir-fry the sprouts for 2 minutes. Remove from the heat and stir half the peanut soy paste into the pan.

4 Transfer to a serving dish. Drizzle with the remaining paste and the tablespoon of soy sauce. Sprinkle with the pine nuts. Serve either warm or cold.

Thai Egg Rolls with Chile Dipping Sauce

You can buy chilled or frozen egg roll skins in Chinese grocery stores and supermarkets.

PREPARATION: 20 MINUTES

COOKING: 10 MINUTES

MAKES 12

2 small zucchini

2 tablespoons peanut oil

2 scallions, thinly sliced

4 shiitake mushrooms, stems removed,
    caps thinly sliced

1^1/$_4$ cups bean sprouts

4 to 6 sprigs each fresh basil, mint, and
    watercress, leaves cut into thin slivers

1 teaspoon dark soy sauce

2 tablespoons mirin (Japanese rice wine), or
    1 tablespoon each dry sherry and water

^{1}/$_2$-inch piece fresh ginger root, minced

12 egg roll skins

1 egg, beaten

Oil for deep-frying

Salt and pepper

FOR THE CHILE DIPPING SAUCE:

1 tablespoon each soy sauce, peanut oil,
    and lime juice

1 small hot chile, seeded and thinly sliced

1 Cut each zucchini across into 8 thick slices; cut each slice into thin sticks.

2 Heat the peanut oil in a skillet. Add the zucchini, onions, mushrooms, bean sprouts, basil, mint, and watercress, and stir-fry with the soy sauce, mirin, and ginger until softened slightly, 1 to 2 minutes. Season to taste.

3 Spoon 1 tablespoon of the mixture on one end of egg roll skin and roll up, folding in the ends and brushing with beaten egg to help it seal. Repeat to make 12.

4 Fill a wok one-third full with oil and heat until a stale bread cube dropped into the oil turns golden brown after about 15 seconds. Alternatively, heat the oil in a deep-fat fryer to 350°F. Deep-fry the rolls, 4 at a time, for 1 to 2 minutes until golden brown, turning from time to time. Remove with a slotted spoon and drain on paper towels.

5 Mix together the dipping sauce ingredients in a bowl.

6 Serve the egg rolls with the dipping sauce.

Green Vegetable Curry with Shiitake Mushrooms

Jars of Thai green curry paste and fresh shiitake mushrooms are sold in supermarkets and some Asian grocery stores.

PREPARATION: 7 MINUTES

COOKING: 10 MINUTES

SERVES 4

1¼ cups coconut milk, plus 2 tablespoons
   more for garnish

3 tablespoons Thai green curry paste

1¼ cups vegetable stock

8 baby eggplants, each halved lengthwise

8 ounces yard-long or French beans, cut into
   1 inch lengths

1 teaspoon muscovado or Turbinado sugar

1 teaspoon Thai fish sauce or soy sauce

1 ounce ginger root, peeled and chopped

4 ounces shiitake mushrooms, sliced

Fresh basil and cilantro leaves, to garnish

1 Heat the 1¼ cups coconut milk in a saucepan with the curry paste. Stir well to combine.

2 Add the stock and then the eggplant, beans, sugar, fish or soy sauce, ginger, and the mushrooms. Bring to a boil and simmer, stirring, for 3 to 4 minutes. Adjust the seasoning with more sugar and fish or soy sauce as necessary.

3 Serve in bowls, garnished with the basil and cilantro leaves and drizzled with the extra coconut milk.

Spicy Green Lentils with Crisp Onions

PREPARATION: 20 MINUTES

COOKING: 45 MINUTES

SERVES 2 AS A MAIN COURSE

WITH PARATHAS (SEE PAGE 144)

Scant 1 cup whole green lentils

¼ teaspoon each ground turmeric, cayenne
pepper, and fenugreek seeds

¼-inch piece fresh ginger root, grated

¾ teaspoon salt

1 tomato, chopped

1 tablespoon ghee or vegetable oil

1 teaspoon cumin seeds

3 whole cloves

3 garlic cloves, minced

1 onion, sliced

¼ teaspoon garam masala

1 tablespoon fresh cilantro leaves

1 Rinse the lentils in a strainer. In a pan, combine the lentils, turmeric, cayenne pepper, fenugreek, ginger, 2½ cups water, and the salt. Bring to a boil. Cover, lower the heat, and simmer for 40 minutes, by which time the water should all be absorbed (if necessary, a little extra water can be added during cooking). Stir in the tomato.

2 Meanwhile, heat the ghee or oil in a skillet. Add the cumin seeds and cloves. When they crackle, add the garlic and onion. When the onion begins to brown and crisp, turn off the heat.

3 Bring the lentils to a slow simmer and quickly add half the fried spice and onion mixture. Sprinkle with the remaining onions, garam masala, and cilantro leaves.

4 Serve with Parathas, if desired.

Cabbage Parathas with Sesame Seeds

In India, normal everyday breads are not flavored because they are eaten with spicy curries, but this north Indian unleavened bread has been mildly spiced, so is more of a snack bread. It goes well with mild-flavored lentil and vegetable dishes.

PREPARATION: 30 MINUTES

COOKING: ABOUT 15 MINUTES

MAKES 8 PARATHAS

$^2/_3$ cup whole wheat flour, plus extra for rolling and dusting

$^2/_3$ cup all-purpose flour

1 cup very finely shredded green cabbage

$^1/_2$-inch piece fresh ginger root, peeled and grated

$^1/_2$ teaspoon cayenne pepper

1 tablespoon sesame seeds

$^1/_4$ teaspoon turmeric

$^1/_2$ teaspoon dill seeds (optional)

1 teaspoon salt

1 tablespoon vegetable oil, extra for brushing

About $^1/_2$ cup warm water

1 In a bowl, combine the flours with the cabbage, ginger root, cayenne, sesame seeds, turmeric, dill seeds (if using), and salt. Stir in the vegetable oil, and gradually add $^1/_2$ cup warm water, mixing everything to make a soft dough; add more water if necessary. Do not add all the water at once because if too much is added the dough will be very sticky and difficult to roll. Divide into 8 equal balls.

2 Heat a cast-iron skillet or griddle until very hot. Flatten each ball and dust with flour. Roll each ball into a 6-inch circle on a chopping board.

3 Slap the paratha on the hot pan and let it cook for 45 to 60 seconds before turning it over. Brush the cooked side with oil, turn over again, and cook for 20 seconds. Brush the second side with oil, turn again, and cook for 20 seconds.

4 Remove from the griddle and put on a plate; keep warm by covering loosely with a dish towel. Repeat with the remaining dough balls. Serve hot or cold.

Cauliflower, Beans, and Tomatoes with Mustard Seeds

PREPARATION: 15 MINUTES

COOKING: 20 MINUTES

SERVES 4

4 tablespoons vegetable oil

1 tablespoon black mustard seeds

1 small onion, minced

3 garlic cloves, minced

$1^1/_2$ cups cauliflower cut into small florets

$1^1/_2$ cups green beans cut into $1^1/_2$-inch pieces

$^1/_2$ teaspoon cayenne pepper

$^1/_2$ teaspoon turmeric

1 teaspoon each salt and sugar

$^1/_2$-inch piece fresh ginger root, grated

12 cherry tomatoes, halved

$^1/_2$ teaspoon garam masala

1 Heat the oil in a skillet. Add the mustard seeds and sauté until they pop. Add the onion and garlic and sauté until golden. Stir in the cauliflower and beans and sauté for 5 minutes until the florets begin to singe.

2 Add the cayenne, turmeric, salt, sugar, and ginger, together with 2 tablespoons of water. Cover and cook slowly for 15 minutes. Add the tomatoes and cook 2 minutes longer.

3 Sprinkle with the garam masala and serve.

Opposite (clockwise from bottom left): Cauliflower, Beans, and Tomatoes with Mustard Seeds; Spicy Green Lentils with Crisp Onions (page 143); Cabbage Parathas with Sesame Seeds

Festive Bites

Vegetables aren't normally the first type of ingredient that comes to mind when thinking of party food, but they are perfect candidates—making the best and most flavorful of dips and providing the most unusual and colorful toppings for canapés. Even the canapé bases can be made from vegetables, as in our mini roasted potatoes with various toppings.

Party Food

Garlic-Sesame Dip with Crisp Pitas

You can buy jars of tahini paste from large supermarkets, as well as health-food stores. The dip can be made the day before and stored in the refrigerator.

PREPARATION: ABOUT 20 MINUTES
BROILING: ABOUT 5 MINUTES
MAKES 50 SCOOPS

4 thick slices of white country-style bread, crusts removed, cut into
    cubes
1 tablespoon tahini paste
2 garlic cloves, crushed
$^3/_4$ cup extra-virgin olive oil
2 tablespoons fromage blanc
Juice of 1 lemon
8 pita breads, split in half
2 teaspoons toasted sesame seeds
Salt and pepper
Selection of olives, to serve

1 Preheat the broiler. Sprinkle the bread with water, then squeeze well and put in a food processor or blender with the tahini and garlic. Process until smooth, drizzling in the oil in a slow steady stream until the mixture forms a thick paste.
2 Transfer to a bowl and stir in the fromage blanc, lemon juice, and salt and pepper to taste.
3 Tear the pita breads into rough pieces. Place on a cookie sheet and broil for 4 to 5 minutes until lightly brown.
4 Sprinkle the dip with sesame seeds and serve with the crisp pitas and olives.

Pakoras with Spicy Yogurt Dip

PREPARATION: 15 MINUTES
COOKING: 12 TO 15 MINUTES
MAKES ABOUT 16

$4^1/_2$ cups mixed vegetables, such as potato, zucchini, bell peppers,
    okra, onion, and eggplant, cut into $^1/_2$-inch cubes
Oil for frying
FOR THE SPICY YOGURT DIP:
1 small onion, quartered
1 garlic clove
$^1/_2$ ounce fresh cilantro
1 red chile, halved and seeded
2 tablespoons blanched almonds
1 tablespoon lime juice
$^2/_3$ cup plain yogurt
Salt and pepper
FOR THE BATTER:
2 garlic cloves, crushed
1 teaspoon each ground cumin, coriander, turmeric, cayenne pepper,
    and salt
2 teaspoons garam masala
1 cup gram flour (chickpea flour)
2 tablespoons sunflower oil
2 tablespoons each chopped fresh mint and cilantro

1 To make the dip, place the onion, garlic, cilantro, chile, almonds, and lime juice in a food processor and process. Stir in the yogurt and season to taste; chill.
2 Mix all the batter ingredients with 1 cup cold water to make a smooth, thick batter. Season to taste.
3 Blanch any hard vegetables, such as carrots or potatoes, in lightly salted boiling water for 2 to 3 minutes; drain well. Stir into the batter with the rest of the vegetables and coat well.
4 Heat $1^1/_2$ inches of oil in a pan until a cube of bread dropped into it rises to the surface and browns within 1 minute. Drop heaped tablespoons of the vegetable mixture into the hot oil and fry in batches for 2 to 3 minutes, turning occasionally, until golden. Drain on paper towels and keep hot.
5 Serve with the spicy yogurt dip.

Hummus

PREPARATION: ABOUT 15 MINUTES

SERVES 4

2 (14 ounce) cans chickpeas, drained

Juice of 1 lemon

3 tablespoons tahini paste (optional)

2 tablespoons olive oil, plus more to serve

2 garlic cloves, crushed

Fresh flat-leaf parsley sprigs, to serve

1 Whirl the chickpeas in a blender or food processor until crumblike.

2 Transfer to a bowl. Beat in the lemon juice, tahini if using, olive oil, and garlic with a wooden spoon. If the mixture seems heavy, add a little water to lighten it.

3 To serve, spoon into small dishes, pour a pool of olive oil in the middle, and garnish with parsley.

Hummus Falafel

PREPARATION: 10 MINUTES

COOKING: 10 MINUTES

MAKES ABOUT 24

1$\frac{1}{2}$ cups prepared hummus, or see above

4 tablespoons ground blanched almonds

3 tablespoons chopped fresh cilantro, plus more leaves to garnish

2 tablespoons lemon juice

Salt and pepper

2 tablespoons olive oil

1 In a bowl, mix together the hummus, almonds, cilantro, and 1 teaspoon of the lemon juice; season to taste.

2 Take 1 tablespoon of the mixture and shape into a 1$\frac{1}{4}$-inch ball; repeat with the remaining mixture.

3 Heat the oil in a skillet and cook the falafel in batches for 2 minutes on each side until golden brown. Drain on paper towels.

4 Served topped with the extra whole cilantro leaves and with the remaining lemon juice sprinkled over.

TOP LEFT TO RIGHT Mushroom Frittata; Mini Crab Tortilla
MIDDLE LEFT TO RIGHT Pâté Crostini with Onion Marmalade; Smoked Salmon
and Horseradish Crostini; Mozzarella with Mediterranean Tomato Salsa
BOTTOM LEFT TO RIGHT Duck with Kumquat and Shallot Relish; Tomato Tartlets
with Pesto; Ham Rarebit with Gherkin Salad; Scallops and Sage Wrapped in Bacon

Canapé Cornucopia

MUSHROOM FRITTATA

MAKES 32

Preheat the broiler to high. Beat together 6 eggs, 3 tablespoons heavy cream, and ¼ cup finely grated Parmesan cheese; season. Heat 2 tablespoons olive oil and 2 tablespoons butter in a small skillet. Add 3½ cups sliced crimini mushrooms and cook for 5 minutes until soft; season. Spread the mushrooms evenly over the pan. Pour the egg mixture over and fry slowly for 5 minutes. Sprinkle another ¼ cup grated Parmesan over the top. Place the pan under the broiler for about 2 minutes until the frittata is puffed and golden on top. Serve hot or cold, cut into small wedges or cubes.

MINI CRAB TORTILLA

MAKES 20

Mix 6 ounces crabmeat (fresh, defrosted frozen, or drained canned) with 2 tablespoons sour cream, 1 tablespoon lime juice, 1 teaspoon hot-pepper sauce, and 1 finely chopped scallion; season. Seed and finely chop 1 pound tomatoes. Spoon a generous amount of crab mixture on each of 20 corn tortilla chips and top with a spoonful of the chopped tomato.

PÂTÉ CROSTINI WITH ONION MARMALADE

MAKES 30

Preheat the oven to 350°F. Cut a baguette into thirty ½-inch slices. Bake for about 10 minutes until golden and crisp; let cool. Meanwhile, heat 2 tablespoons olive oil in a skillet. Add 3 thinly sliced red onions, 2 teaspoons sugar, 3 tablespoons balsamic vinegar, ½ teaspoon ground star anise or five-spice powder, and pinch of dried thyme. Cook slowly, stirring occasionally, for 30 minutes until soft and caramelized; let cool. To serve, place a small portion of coarse pâté (7 ounces in total) on each toast and top with the onion marmalade.

SMOKED SALMON AND HORSERADISH CROSTINI

MAKES 30

Preheat the oven to 350°F. Slice a baguette and bake as for the crostini above; set aside to cool. Beat together 7 tablespoons each crème fraîche or sour cream and prepared horseradish with 1 teaspoon each grated lemon zest and honey. Put a spoonful of mixture on each crostini, top with coil of smoked salmon (9 ounces in total), and garnish with dill sprigs to serve.

MOZZARELLA WITH MEDITERRANEAN TOMATO SALSA

MAKES 30

Heat 2 tablespoons olive oil in a small pan. Add 1 teaspoon fennel seeds and heat slowly for 1 minute. Remove from heat and stir in 1 teaspoon dried oregano; let cool. Stir 6 seeded and chopped plum tomatoes, 10 halved pitted ripe olives, and 1 tablespoon chopped parsley into the cooled oil; season. Cut 18 ounces fresh mozzarella cheese into thirty ¼-inch slices and thinly slice ½ red onion. Top each slice of mozzarella with a spoonful of tomato salsa and 2 or 3 onion slices. Serve at room temperature.

DUCK WITH KUMQUAT AND SHALLOT RELISH

MAKES 30

The day before, rub 2 trimmed duck legs with salt and 1 tablespoon five-spice powder. Place in a plastic bag. Mix 1 tablespoon each dark soy sauce and honey with 2 teaspoons dark sesame oil. Pour over duck in bag, seal, and chill overnight. Next day, preheat the oven to 350°F. In a small pan, slowly heat 6 tablespoons olive oil with 1 bruised garlic clove for a few minutes; leave to cool with garlic in. Slice a baguette, brush with the garlic-infused oil and bake as for crostini; let cool. Increase the oven to 400°F and roast the duck for 50 minutes. Let cool, then shred meat from bones. Make the relish by heating 2 tablespoons olive oil in a small pan. Add 8 quartered small shallots, 1 small finely chopped red onion, and 3 chopped garlic cloves. Cook for 5 minutes until golden. Add $^1/_2$ tablespoon sugar and 2 tablespoons red wine vinegar and cook until reduced and caramelized. Add another tablespoon sugar and 10 kumquats, each cut into 8 wedges, with the juice of 2 oranges and 5 tablespoons water; season. Bring to a simmer and simmer for 15 minutes until reduced to a relish consistency. Top each toast with a little relish and some shredded duck. Garnish with chicory.

TOMATO TARTLETS WITH PESTO

MAKES 25

Preheat the oven to 425°F. Roll out 9 ounces puff pastry dough to a thickness of $^1/_4$-inch. Stamp out 25 circles, slightly larger than the small tomatoes you are using; place on a cookie sheet. Cut each of 5 tomatoes into 5 slices and place one on each dough circle. Brush the tartlets with beaten egg. Bake for 10 to 12 minutes until risen and golden. Top each tartlet with 1 teaspoon of pesto. Serve warm.

HAM RAREBIT WITH GHERKIN SALAD

MAKES 30

Preheat the oven to 400°F. Slice a baguette as for the crostini on the previous page. Mix together 2 tablespoons olive oil, 3 tablespoons softened butter, and 2 tablespoons whole-grain mustard. Brush over both sides of each baguette slice and bake for 8 minutes until crisp. Make the gherkin salad by mixing 10 finely chopped gherkins, 2 finely chopped shallots, and 1 tablespoon olive oil. Preheat the broiler to high. Top each toast with a piece of thinly sliced ham ($2^1/_2$ ounces in total), then a wafer-thin shaving of cheddar ($3^1/_2$ ounces in total). Season and broil until the cheese melts. Top with a spoonful of gherkin salad to serve.

SCALLOPS AND SAGE WRAPPED IN BACON

MAKES 20

Preheat the oven to 400°F. Place a sage leaf on top of each of 20 medium scallops (or 10 large, cut horizontally into 2 slices). Stretch 20 slices of smoked bacon with the back of a knife; cut each in half lengthwise. Wrap a bacon strip around each scallop, and then wrap another around, across the first to enclose the scallop completely. Brush with garlic-infused oil (see the Duck with Kumquat recipe, left). Bake for 10 to 12 minutes until crisp. Serve speared with toothpicks.

Vegetable Skewers

PREPARATION: ABOUT 30 MINUTES
BAKING: ABOUT 30 MINUTES
MAKES 25

2 red bell peppers, cored and seeded but left whole
1 butternut squash, peeled, halved, seeded, and cut lengthwise into $^1/_2$-inch slices
$^1/_2$ cup olive oil
2 garlic cloves, crushed
1 teaspoon each ground coriander and paprika
1 eggplant, sliced lengthwise
5 ounces soft goat cheese
2 teaspoons toasted cumin seeds
25 woody rosemary sprigs (optional)
Salt and pepper

1 Preheat the oven to 425°F. Put the peppers and squash slices on a cookie sheet. In a bowl, mix the oil, garlic, coriander, paprika, and seasoning together. Brush the mixture over the squash. Bake for 15 minutes until the squash is tender.
2 Transfer the squash to a plate. Put the peppers in a plastic bag and seal; let cool.
3 Put the eggplant slices on a cookie sheet, brush with some oil mixture, and bake for 10 minutes; set aside to cool.
4 Spread the cheese all over half the eggplant slices and sprinkle with cumin seeds. Sandwich with the remaining eggplant slices. Cut the sandwiches and squash slices into 10 × $1^1/_4$ inch squares.
5 Peel the skins off the peppers and cut the flesh into 10 × $1^1/_4$ inch squares.
6 Layer the vegetables, alternating the colors. Spear with a rosemary sprig or toothpick and place on a cookie sheet. Brush with the remaining oil mix and bake for 3 to 5 minutes. Serve warm.

Mini Roasted Potatoes

Small or new potatoes are ideal for roasting and topping, served warm as canapés.

PREPARATION: 30 MINUTES
BAKING: 30 TO 40 MINUTES
MAKES 16 PIECES

WHAT YOU DO

Preheat the oven to 375°F. Toss 8 small potatoes in 2 tablespoons olive oil and place in a roasting pan. Sprinkle with coarse sea salt and freshly ground black pepper. Roast for 30 to 40 minutes until tender. Leave the potatoes to stand until they are cool enough to handle; split them in half lengthwise.

MAKE AHEAD

Cook the potatoes up to 2 hours ahead, but don't cut them in half; let them cool completely. Cover and store in the refrigerator. Warm through before serving, or serve at room temperature.

THE TOPPINGS:
INSTANT CORONATION CHICKEN

Put 2 tablespoons roughly chopped cooked chicken in a bowl with 1 tablespoon chopped, seeded red bell pepper. Stir in 1 tablespoon fromage blanc, 1 teaspoon curry paste, 2 teaspoons mango chutney, and 1 tablespoon chopped fresh parsley. Carefully spoon onto 4 potato halves. Cover and chill until needed.

BLUE CHEESE AND CHIVES

Crumble 1 ounce blue cheese and divide among 4 potato halves. Sprinkle 1 tablespoon snipped fresh chives over. Just before serving, broil for 1 to 2 minutes until the cheese is bubbling.

SMOKED SALMON AND HORSERADISH

Mix 1 teaspoon horseradish sauce with 1 tablespoon crème fraîche and divide among 4 potato halves. Tear 1 ounce smoked salmon into 8 pieces; put 2 on top of each potato half. Cover and chill until needed.

CRÈME FRAÎCHE AND SCALLION

Season 2 tablespoons crème fraîche with salt and pepper. Divide among 4 potato halves. Chop 2 scallions and sprinkle over the potatoes. Cover and chill. Just before serving, sprinkle with a little freshly ground black pepper.

Acknowledgments

Recipes by

Sue Ashworth
New vegetables à la grecque p26, Three-bean salad with citrus dressing p54, Roasted vegetable quiche p69

Lindsey Bareham
Feta and herb briouats p29, Potatoes sautéed with garlic and onion p124

Annie Bell
Warm salad of roasted eggplant, tomatoes and cannellini beans p34

Angela Boggiano
Simple curried vegetable broth p13, Grilled sweet potato and beet salad p49, Shallot tatin p75, Vegetable lasagna p83, Roasted stuffed onions p88, Basic baked potato p116, Blue cheese and herb potatoes p116, Spinach, mushroom, and egg potatoes p116, Hummus and avocado salsa potatoes p116, Eggplant chile potatoes p116, Spiced roasted potatoes p119, Roasted potatoes p120, Red onion, garlic, and rosemary roasties p121, Hasselback potatoes p122, Pan haggerty p127, Potato rösti p128, Soufflé potatoes p130, French fries p131, Basic mashed potatoes p132, Aligot p132, Leek and mustard mashed potatoes p132, Herb and Parmesan mashed potatoes p132, Colcannon p132, Clapshot p132, Champ p132, Hummus falafel p149

Lorna Brash
Caldo verde p10, Honeyed carrot and fig couscous p32, Tricolor muffins p44, Tarragon mushrooms with bean mashed potatoes p47, Summer vegetable lattice tart p69, Polenta-squash layer p81, Char-grilled vegetable pasticcio p98, Marinated couscous with harissa tomatoes p99, Pakoras with spicy yogurt dip p148

Mary Cadogan
Spicy gazpacho with basil p10, Mozzarella pasta with olives and chile p100, Leek and blue cheese risotto p104

Robert Carrier
Tomato stacks with herb and onion salsa p31, Thai spring rolls with chile dipping sauce p142

Gilly Cubitt
Stoved new potatoes and mushrooms p127, Vegetable stir-fry with phyllo "noodles" p139

Lewis Esson
Vegetable stock p17, Green vegetable curry with shiitake mushrooms p143

Joanna Farrow
Mushroom-wonton soup p14, Warm maple-glazed vegetable salad with feta and walnuts p50

Ursula Ferrigno
Fennel raviolini pp94-5, Fennel raviolini with roasted vegetable and saffron sauce p97

Rebecca Ford
Chinese broth with curly kale seaweed p12, Asparagus with lime and cilantro butter p36, Potato cakes with chard and hollandaise p44, Tomato and oregano pizza p113, Pimiento, arugula, and mozzarella pizza p113

Silvana Franco
Creamy mushroom lasagna p82, Cheesy spaghetti with zucchini and bacon p92, Spicy pepper penne p98

Paul Gayler
Chestnut gnocchi with sour cranberries p107, Potato latkes with herb-broiled feta p128

Susanna Gelmetti
Fennel risotto p104, Pizza crust pp108-9, Pizza toppings p110-1

The Good Food Team
Chickpea and tomato broth p23, Feta and anchovy stuffed peppers p26, Eggplant and mozzarella stacks p30, Vegetable omelet p35, Asparagus and soft egg tartlets p38, Roasted asparagus with poached eggs p38, Roasted ham and mushroom toast p40, Garlicky mushroom toasts p43, Butter bean, olive, and feta salad p61, Caesar salad with Parmesan chips p62, Goat cheese and onion tartlets p72, Leek, ham and Camembert gratin p79, Pasta with broccoli and toasted nuts p92, Tomato and mushroom stacks p100, Oven egg and fries p119

Clare Gordon-Smith
Vegetable patties with spicy tomato chutney p31, from her book, Flavouring with Chiles (Ryland, Peters & Small). Reprinted by permission of the Peters Fraser and Dunlop Group Limited on behalf of the author.

Peter Gorton
Spiced lentil soup with lemon yogurt p13, Baked goat cheese bundles with sweet-and-sour leeks p27, from his restaurant, The Horn of Plenty, Devon

Mark Gregory
Udon noodles with miso and roasted ginger pumpkin p136, from his restaurant t'su, London

Jane Grigson
Spicy parsnip soup p16, from her book, Jane Grigson's Vegetable Book (Penguin Books)

Sophie Grigson
Roasted squash with lime and caper sauce p88, Spaghetti alla puttanesca p93

Alastair Hendy
Roasted vine tomatoes and onions with cheddar p40, Mushrooms with truffle oil on Italian country toast p40, Spicy avocado and cilantro on corn bread toast p40, Garlic-sesame dip with crisp pitas p148, Mushroom frittata p151, Mini crab tortilla p151, Pâté crostini with onion marmalade p151, Smoked salmon and horseradish crostini p151, Mozzarella with Mediterranean tomato salsa p151, Duck with kumquat and shallot relish p152, Tomato tartlets with pesto p152, Ham rarebit with gherkin salad p152, Scallops and sage wrapped in bacon p152, Vegetable skewers p152

Ken Hom
Vegetable salad with curry-soy vinaigrette p54, from his book, Travels with a Hot Wok (BBC Books)

Sybil Kapoor
Hoisin Chinese noodles p138

Orlando Murrin
Jerusalem artichoke soup p22, Sausage-stuffed cabbage p84, Roman spinach p102

Angela Nilsen
Old-Fashioned tomato sauce p20, Cherry tomato and basil clafoutis p47, Salad dressings pp56-7, French onion tart p73, Tomato tarte tatin p75, Chile oil p140

Meena Pathak
Spicy green lentils with crisp onions p143, Cabbage parathas with sesame seeds p144, Cauliflower, beans, and tomatoes with mustard seeds p144

Gary Rhodes
Warm poached eggs on potato salad p49, Asparagus, sea kale, and red onion salad with spicy potato croutons and sour cream and chive dressing p61, Macaroni and cheese pies with artichokes and mushrooms p66, provençale tartlets with pesto sauce p70

Lyn Rutherford
Mediterranean salad p62

Bridget Sargeson
Velvety cauliflower-cheese soup p19, Minty pea and ham soup p19

Vanessa Scott
Goat cheese and olive toasts p43

Bill Sewell
Leek and potato pie p67, from his restaurants The Place Below, London, and Café@All Saints, Hereford

Mary Spyrou
Hummus p149

Carla Tomasi
Piedmontese peppers p50

Linda Tubby
Goat cheese polenta with mushrooms p32, Scalloped potato and rich cheese tart p122, Brussels sprouts with peanut sauce p142

The Vegetarian Good Food Team
Chilled beet soup with horseradish cream p22, Carrot and potato flat bread p79

Becca Watson
Fiorelli with oven-dried vegetables and tapenade p97, from her book, Perfect Pasta (Merehurst Ltd)

Jenny White
Salted beans p52, Spinach and Gruyère tart p73, Jerusalem artichoke and mushroom dauphinoise p76, Polenta, red pepper, and zucchini gratin p80, Cabbage rolls with roasted ratatouille p86, Mini roasted potatoes p154

Antony Worrall Thompson
Dandelion leaves with pear, Roquefort, and hazelnuts p58

Peter Wright
French lentil salad p59, Tamari and toasted seed coleslaw p59, Tian of zucchini p81

Photographers

William Adams-Lingwood
Piedmontese peppers p50

Marie-Louise Avery
Roasted squash with lime and caper sauce p89, Spaghetti alla puttanesca p93, Roasted potatoes step-by-steps pp120-1, Hummus p149

Martin Brigdale
Mushroom-wonton soup pp14-5, Warm maple-glazed vegetable salad with feta and walnuts p51, Salad dressing step-by-steps p56, Salad p57, Roasted vegetable quiche p68

Robin Broadbent
Provençale tartlets with pesto sauce p71

Peter Cassidy
Chestnut gnocchi with sour cranberries p106, Udon noodles with miso and roasted ginger pumpkin p137

Jean Cazals
Old-fashioned tomato sauce p20, Tomatoes p21, Cherry tomato and basil clafoutis p46, Salted beans p52, Runner beans p53, Tomato tarte tatin p74, Mozzarella pasta with olives and chile p101, Fennel risotto p104, Pizza toppings pp110-1, Chiles p140, Chile oil p141

Mick Dean
Spicy parsnip soup step-by-steps pp16-7

Ken Field
Tricolor muffins p45, Hoisin Chinese noodles p138

Gus Filgate
Leek and potato pie p67

David Jordan
Caldo verde p11, French lentil salad p59

Dave King
Baked goat cheese bundles with sweet-and-sour leeks p27

Graham Kirk
Velvety cauliflower-cheese soup p18

Jess Koppel
Grilled sweet potato and beet salad p49, Roasted stuffed onions p88

Sandra Lane
Brussels sprouts with peanut sauce p142

David Munns
Sausage-stuffed cabbage p84, Cabbage p85, Roman spinach p102, Spinach p103

James Murphy
Asparagus and soft egg tartlets p38

Thomas Odulate
Fennel raviolini step-by-steps pp94-5, Fennel raviolini with roasted vegetable and saffron sauce p96, Potato latkes with herb-broiled feta p129

William Reavell
Chinese broth with curly kale seaweed p12, Potato cakes with chard and hollandaise p44, Stoved new potatoes and mushrooms p127, Vegetable stir-fry with phyllo "noodles" p139

Roger Stowell
Spicy gazpacho with basil p8, Jerusalem artichoke soup p22, Chickpea and tomato broth p23, Roasted vegetable omelet p35, Spicy avocado on cilantro corn bread toast p40, Roasted ham and mushroom toast p40, Mushrooms with truffle oil on Italian country toast p40, Roasted vine tomatoes and onions with cheddar p41, Warm poached eggs on potato salad p48, Butter bean, olive, and feta salad p61, Caesar salad with Parmesan chips p63, Macaroni and cheese pies with artichokes and mushrooms p64, Leek, ham, and camembert gratin p78, Polenta, red pepper and zucchini gratin p80, Pasta with broccoli and toasted nuts p90, Basic baked potato p114, Blue cheese and herb potatoes p116, Spinach, mushroom and egg potatoes p116, Eggplant chile potatoes p116, Hummus and avocado salsa potatoes p117, Oven egg and fries p118, Spiced roasted potatoes p119, Red onion, garlic, and rosemary roasties p121, Hasselback potatoes p122, Pan haggerty p126, Potato rösti p128, Soufflè potatoes p130, French fries p131, Aligot p132, Leek and mustard mashed potatoes p132, Herb and Parmesan mashed potatoes p132, Basic mashed potato p133, Spring vegetable noodles p134, Cauliflower, beans and tomatoes with mustard seeds p145, Garlic-sesame dip with crisp pitas p146, Canapés pp150-1, Grilled vegetable and goat cheese skewers p153

Sam Stowell
Dandelion leaves with pear, Roquefort, and hazelnuts p58, Jerusalem artichoke and mushroom dauphinoise p76, Artichokes p77

Martin Thompson
Creamy mushroom lasagna p82

Trevor Vaughan
Marinated couscous with harissa tomatoes p99

Philip Webb
Feta and Piedmontese peppers p24, Feta and herb briouats p28, Feta and herb briouats (detail) p29, Eggplant and mozzarella stacks p30, Eggplant and mozzarella stacks (detail) p30, Goat cheese polenta with mushrooms p33, Warm salad of roasted eggplant, tomatoes, and cannellini beans p34, Asparagus p37, Roasted asparagus with poached eggs p39, Garlicky mushroom toasts p42, Three-bean salad with citrus dressing p55, Goat cheese and onion tartlets p72, Goat cheese and onion tartlets step-by-step p72, Cabbage rolls with roasted ratatouille p86, Scalloped potato and rich cheese tart p123, Potatoes sautéed with garlic and onion p124, Potatoes p125, Mini roasted potatoes pp154-5

Simon Wheeler
Leek and blue cheese risotto p105

Frank Wieder
Asparagus with lime and cilantro butter p36, Summer vegetable lattice tart p69, Tomato and oregano pizza p112

Geoff Wilkinson
Pizza crust step-by-steps pp108-9

While every effort has been made to trace and acknowledge all copyright holders, we would like to apologize should there be any errors or omissions.

Index

A

aligot, 132

anchovies:
  spaghetti alla puttanesca, 93

appetizers, 25-62

artichokes, macaroni and
    cheese pies with
    mushrooms and, 66

arugula: pimiento, arugula and
    mozzarella pizza, 113
  pizza con rucola, 111

asparagus, 36
  asparagus and soft egg
    tartlets, 38
  asparagus with lime and
    cilantro butter, 36
  asparagus, sea kale and red
    onion salad, 61
  roasted asparagus with
    poached eggs, 38

avocados:
  hummus and avocado salsa
    potatoes, 116
  spicy avocado on cilantro
    corn bread toast, 40

B

beans:
  caldo verde, 10
  tarragon mushrooms with
    bean mashed potatoes, 47
  three-bean salad with citrus
    dressing, 54
  warm salad of roasted
    eggplant, tomatoes, and
    cannellini beans, 34

bean sprouts:
  Thai egg rolls with chile
    dipping sauce, 142

beet:
  chilled beet soup with
    horseradish cream, 22
  grilled sweet potato and
    beet salad, 49

bread:
  carrot and potato flat bread, 79
  cabbage parathas with
    sesame seeds, 144

briouats, feta and herb, 29

broccoli, pasta with toasted
    nuts and, 92

Brussels sprouts with peanut
    sauce, 142

butter, lime and cilantro, 36

butter bean, olive and feta
    salad, 61

C

cabbage, 84
  cabbage parathas with
    sesame seeds, 144
  cabbage rolls with roasted
    ratatouille, 86
  caldo verde, 10
  colcannon, 132
  sausage-stuffed cabbage, 84
  tamari and toasted seed
    coleslaw, 59

Caesar salad with Parmesan
    chips, 62

caldo verde, 10

canapés, 151

cannellini beans:
  caldo verde, 10
  warm salad of roasted
    eggplant, tomatoes, and, 34

carrots:
  carrot and potato flat bread,
    79
  honeyed carrot and fig
    couscous, 32

cauliflower:
  cauliflower, beans, and
    tomatoes with mustard
    seeds, 144
  velvety cauliflower-cheese
    soup, 19

champ, 132

chard, potato cakes with
    hollandaise and, 44

cheese:
  aligot, 132
  baked goat cheese bundles,
    27
  blue cheese and chives
    topping, 154
  blue cheese and herb
    potatoes, 116
  butter bean, olive, and feta
    salad, 61
  char-grilled vegetable
    pasticcio, 98
  cheesy spaghetti with
    zucchini and bacon, 92
  creamy mushroom
    lasagna, 82
  dandelion leaves with pear,
    Roquefort and hazelnuts, 58

eggplant and mozzarella
    stacks, 30

fennel raviolini, 94-7

feta and anchovy stuffed
    peppers, 26

feta and herb briouats, 29

goat cheese and olive
    toasts, 43

goat cheese and onion
    tartlets, 72

goat cheese polenta with
    mushrooms, 32

leek and blue cheese
    risotto, 104

leek and potato pie, 67

leek, ham and Camembert
    gratin, 79

macaroni and cheese pies
    with artichokes and
    mushrooms, 66

mozzarella pasta with olives
    and chile, 100

mozzarella with
    Mediterranean tomato
    salsa, 151

Parmesan crisps, 62

pimiento, arugula and
    mozzarella pizza, 113

pizza al funghi e ricotta, 111

pizza bianca con semi de
    finocchio e formaggio, 110

polenta, red pepper, and
    zucchini gratin, 80

polenta-squash layer, 81

potato latkes with
    herb-broiled feta, 128

roasted vine tomatoes and
    onions with cheddar, 40

scalloped potato and rich
    cheese tart, 122

spinach and Gruyère tart, 73

vegetable lasagna, 83

velvety cauliflower-cheese
    soup, 19

warm maple-glazed
    vegetable salad with feta
    and walnuts, 50

cherry tomato and basil
    clafoutis, 47

chestnut gnocchi with sour
    cranberries, 107

chicken:
  instant coronation
    chicken topping, 154

chickpeas:
  chickpea and tomato broth, 23
  hummus, 149

chiles, 140

Chinese broth with curly kale
    seaweed, 12

chutney, spicy tomato, 31

clafoutis, cherry tomato and
    basil, 47

clapshot, 132

colcannon, 132

coleslaw, tamari and toasted
    seed, 59

couscous:
  honeyed carrot and fig, 32
  marinated couscous with
    harissa tomatoes, 99

crab tortilla, 151

cranberries, chestnut gnocchi
    with, 107

crème fraîche and scallion
    topping, 154

crostini, 151

curry:
  curry-soy vinaigrette, 54
  green vegetable curry, 143
  simple curried vegetable
    broth, 13

D

dandelion leaves with pear,
    Roquefort, and hazelnuts, 58

dips, 148-9

dressings, 56

duck with kumquat and
    shallot relish, 152

E

eggplants:
  eggplant and mozzarella
    stacks, 30
  eggplant-chile potatoes, 116
  green vegetable curry, 143
  tricolor muffins, 44
  warm salad of roasted
    eggplant, tomatoes, and
    cannellini beans, 34

egg rolls, Thai, with chile
    dipping sauce, 142

eggs:
  asparagus and soft egg
    tartlets, 38
  mushroom frittata, 151
  oven egg and fries, 119

roasted asparagus with
    poached eggs, 38

vegetable omelet, 35

warm poached eggs on
    potato salad, 49

F

falafel, hummus, 149

fava beans:
  three-bean salad with citrus
    dressing, 54

fennel:
  fennel raviolini, 94-7
  fennel risotto, 104

feta and anchovy stuffed
    peppers, 26

feta and herb briouats, 29

fiorelli with oven-dried
    vegetables and tapenade, 97

flageolet beans:
  tarragon mushrooms with
    bean mashed potatoes, 47

French lentil salad, 59

French fries, 131

French onion tart, 73

French-style green beans:
  three-bean salad with citrus
    dressing, 54

frittata, mushroom, 151

G

garlic-sesame dip with crisp
    pitas, 148

gazpacho with basil, 10

gherkin salad, 152

gnocchi, chestnut, 107

goat cheese see cheese

green beans, 52
  cauliflower, beans and
    tomatoes with mustard
    seeds, 144
  salted beans, 52

green vegetable curry, 143

H

ham:
  ham rarebit with gherkin
    salad, 152
  leek, ham, and Camembert
    gratin, 79
  minty pea and ham soup, p19
  roasted ham and mushroom
    toast, 40

hasselback potatoes, 122

hoisin Chinese noodles, 138
hollandaise sauce, 44
hummus, 149
  hummus and avocado salsa
    jackets, 116
  hummus falafel, 149

J
Jerusalem artichokes, 76
  Jerusalem artichoke and
    mushroom dauphinoise, 76
  Jerusalem artichoke soup, 22

K
kale:
  curly kale seaweed, 12
kumquat and shallot relish,
  152

L
lasagna:
  creamy mushroom
    lasagna, 82
  vegetable lasagna, 83
latkes, potato, 128
leeks: baked goat cheese
    bundles with sweet-and-
    sour leeks, 27
  leek and blue cheese risotto, 104
  leek and mustard mashed
    potatoes, 132
  leek and potato pie, 67
  leek, ham, and Camembert
    gratin, 79
  pizza con porri e pepe nero,
    111
lentils:
  French lentil salad, 59
  spiced lentil soup with
    lemon yogurt, 13
  spicy green lentils with
    crisp onions, 143

M
macaroni and cheese pies
    with artichokes and
    mushrooms, 66
maple-glazed vegetable
  salad, 50
Mediterranean salad, 62
mozzarella see cheese
muffins, tricolor, 44
mushrooms:
  creamy mushroom lasagna, 82

garlicky mushroom toasts,
  43
goat cheese polenta with
  mushrooms, 32
green vegetable curry with
  shiitake mushrooms, 143
Jerusalem artichoke and
  mushroom dauphinoise, 76
mushroom frittata, 151
mushrooms with truffle oil,
  40
mushroom-wonton soup, 14
pizza al funghi e ricotta, 111
roasted ham and mushroom
  toast, 40
spinach, mushroom, and egg
  potatoes, 116
stoved new potatoes and
  mushrooms, 127
tarragon mushrooms with
  bean mashed potatoes,
  47
tomato and mushroom
  stacks, 100
noodles:
  hoisin Chinese noodles, 138
  spring vegetable noodles, 136
  udon noodles with miso and
    roasted ginger pumpkin,
    136
  vegetable stir-fry with phyllo
    "noodles," 139

O
oils:
  chile oil, 140
  salad dressings, 56
olives, mozzarella pasta with chile
  and, 100
omelet, vegetable, 35
onions:
  French onion tartlets,
    73
  goat cheese and onion
    tartlets, 72
  pâté crostini with onion
    marmalade, 151
  red onion, garlic, and
    rosemary roasties, 121
  roasted stuffed onions, 88
  spicy green lentils with
    crisp onions, 143
  summer vegetable lattice
    pie, 69

P
pakoras with spicy yogurt
  dip, 148
pan haggerty, 127
parathas, cabbage, 144
Parmesan chips, 62
parsnip soup, spicy, 16
party food, 147-54
pasta, 92-100
pastries:
  feta and herb briouats, 29
  pâté crostini with onion
    marmalade, 151
  patties, vegetable, 31
pears: dandelion leaves with
    pear, Roquefort, and
    hazelnuts, 58
peas:
  minty pea and ham soup, 19
penne:
  mozzarella pasta with olives
    and chile, 100
  spicy pepper penne, 98
peppers:
  feta and anchovy stuffed
    peppers, 26
  Mediterranean salad, 62
  Piedmontese peppers, 50
  polenta, red pepper and
    zucchini gratin, 80
  provençale tartlets with pesto
    sauce, 70
  roasted vegetable quiche,
    69
  spicy pepper penne, 98
  summer vegetable lattice
    pie, 69
pesto:
  provençale tartlets with pesto
    sauce, 70
  tomato tartlets with pesto, 152
Piedmontese peppers, 50
pies:
  leek and potato 67
  macaroni and cheese pies
    with artichokes and
    mushrooms, 66
  summer vegetable lattice
    tart, 69
pimiento, arugula and
    mozzarella pizza, 113
pitas, garlic-sesame dip with,
    148
pizzas, 108-13

polenta:
  goat cheese polenta with
    mushrooms, 32
  polenta, red pepper and
    zucchini gratin, 80
  polenta-squash layer, 81
  tomato and mushroom
    stacks, 100
potatoes, 115-32
  aligot, 132
  baked potatoes, 116
  carrot and potato flat bread, 79
  champ, 132
  chestnut gnocchi with sour
    cranberries, 107
  chickpea and tomato broth, 23
  clapshot, 132
  colcannon, 132
  French fries, 131
  hasselback potatoes, 122
  herb and Parmesan mashed
    potatoes, 132
  leek and mustard mashed
    potatoes, 132
  leek and potato pie, 67
  leek, ham, and Camembert
    gratin, 79
  mashed potatoes, 132
  mini roasted potatoes, 154
  oven egg and fries, 119
  pan haggerty, 127
  potato cakes with chard and
    hollandaise, 44
  potato latkes with
    herb-broiled feta, 128
  potato rösti, 128
  potatoes sautéed with garlic
    and onion, 124
  red onion, garlic, and
    rosemary roasties, 121
  roasted potatoes, 120
  scalloped potato and rich
    cheese tart, 122
  soufflé potatoes, 130
  spiced roasted potatoes, 119
  stoved new potatoes and
    mushrooms, 127
  warm poached eggs on
    potato salad, 49
provençale tartlets with pesto
    sauce, 70
pumpkin: udon noodles
    with miso and roasted
    ginger pumpkin, 136

Q
quiche, roasted vegetable, 69

R
ratatouille, cabbage rolls
    with roasted, 86
raviolini, fennel, 94-7
rice:
  cabbage rolls with roasted
    ratatouille, 86
  fennel risotto, 104
  leek and blue cheese
    risotto, 104
risotto see rice
Roman spinach, 102
rösti, potato, 128
runner beans, 52
  salted beans, 52
  three-bean salad with citrus
    dressing, 54
rutabagas:
  clapshot, 132

S
salad dressings, 56
salads:
  asparagus, sea kale and red
    onion salad, 61
  butter bean, olive, and feta
    salad, 61
  Caesar salad with Parmesan
    chips, 62
  French lentil salad, 59
  grilled sweet potato and
    beet salad, 49
  Mediterranean salad, 62
  tamari and toasted seed
    coleslaw, 59
  three-bean salad with citrus
    dressing, 54
  vegetable salad with
    curry-soy vinaigrette, 54
  warm maple-glazed
    vegetable salad with feta
    and walnuts, 50
  warm poached eggs on
    potato salad, 49
  warm salad of roasted
    eggplant, tomatoes, and
    cannellini beans, 34
salted beans, 52
sauces:
  caper sauce, 88
  hollandaise, 44

sauce vierge, 56
sausage-stuffed cabbage, 84
scallions:
   champ, 132
   crème fraîche and scallion topping, 154
scalloped potato and rich cheese tart, 122
scallops and sage wrapped in bacon, 152
sea kale:
   asparagus, sea kale, and red onion salad, 61
seaweed, curly kale, 12
seeds:
   tamari and toasted seed coleslaw, 59
   sesame seeds, cabbage parathas with, 144
shallot Tatin, 75
skewers, vegetable, 152
smoked salmon and horseradish crostini, 151
smoked salmon and horseradish topping, 154
soufflé potatoes, 130
soups, 10-23
spaghetti: cheesy spaghetti with zucchini and bacon, 92
   pasta with broccoli and toasted nuts, 92
   spaghetti alla puttanesca, 93
spinach, 102
   spinach and Gruyère tart, 73
   spinach, mushroom and egg potatoes, 116
   Roman spinach, 102
spring vegetable noodles, 136
squash:
   polenta-squash layer, 81
   roasted squash with lime and caper sauce, 88
stock, vegetable, 17
stoved new potatoes and mushrooms, 127
summer vegetable lattice tart, 69
sweet potatoes:
   grilled sweet potato and beet salad, 49

spiced roasted potatoes, 119

T
tagliatelle:
   char-grilled vegetable pasticcio, 98
tamari and toasted seed coleslaw, 59
tarts:
   asparagus and soft egg tartlets, 38
   French onion tart, 73
   goat cheese and onion tartlets, 72
   provençale tartlets with pesto sauce, 70
   roasted vegetable quiche, 69
   scalloped potato and rich cheese tart, 122
   shallot Tatin, 75
   spinach and Gruyère tart, 73
   tomato tarte Tatin, 75
   tomato tartlets with pesto, 152
Thai egg rolls with chile dipping sauce, 142
tian of zucchini, 81
toasts, 40-3
tofu:
   vegetable stir-fry with phyllo "noodles," 139
tomatoes, 20
   cherry tomato and basil clafoutis, 47
   chickpea and tomato broth, 23
   marinated couscous with harissa tomatoes, 99
   mozzarella with Mediterranean tomato salsa, 151
   pizza Napoletana, 110
   roasted vine tomatoes and onions with cheddar, 40
   sauce, 20
   spicy gazpacho with basil, 10
   tomato and mushroom stacks, 100
   tomato and oregano pizza, 113
   tomato stacks, 31
   tomato tarte Tatin, 75
   tomato tartlets with pesto, 152
   vegetable patties with spicy tomato chutney, 31

warm salad of roasted eggplant, tomatoes, and cannellini beans, 34
tortilla, mini crab, 151
tricolor muffins, 44

U
udon noodles with miso and roasted ginger pumpkin, 136

V
vegetables:
   char-grilled vegetable pasticcio, 98
   Chinese broth with curly kale seaweed, 12
   fiorelli with oven-dried vegetables and tapenade, 97
   hoisin Chinese noodles, 138
   new vegetables à la Grecque, 26
   simple curried vegetable broth, 13
   spring vegetable noodles, 136
   vegetable lasagna, 83
   vegetable omelet, 35
   vegetable patties with spicy tomato chutney, 31
   vegetable skewers, 152
   vegetable stir-fry with phyllo "noodles," 139
   vegetable stock, 17
   see also individual vegetables and salads
vinaigrette, curry-soy, 54
vinegar:
   salad dressings, 56

W
wonton soup, mushroom-, 14

Y
yogurt dip, spicy, 148

Z
zucchini:
   cheesy spaghetti with bacon and, 92
   pizza con menta zucchine, 110
   roasted vegetable quiche, 69
   tian of zucchini, 81